Discovering Your Spiritual *DNA*

THE GOD-GIVEN GIFTS WITHIN YOU ARE THERE FOR A PURPOSE!

But the natural man does not receive the things of the Spirit of God, for they are foolishness to him; nor can he know them, because they are spiritually discerned.
(1 Corinthians 2:14, NKJV)

DR. PETER WOLLENSACK

Discovering Your Spiritual DNA
©2014 by Peter Wollensack

Published by
Harvest Equippers International
Hamden, CT 06514
United States of America
www.harvestequippers.com

ISBN: 978-1-936443-00-0

All Scripture quotations, unless otherwise indicated, are taken from the King James Version of the Bible.

Abbreviations for other Bible versions cited are:

AMP – Amplified Bible / CEV – Contemporary English Version / GNB – Good News Bible / GW – God's Word / HCSB – Holman Christian Standard Bible / NASB – New American Standard Bible / NIV – New International Version / NIRV– New International Reader's Version / NKJV – New King James Version / NLT – New Living Translation/ PNT – J.B. Phillips New Testament

cover design: CJ McDaniel ~ *www.Adazing.com*
book design: Jeff Doles ~ *www.ChristianBookDesign.com*

For bulk order purchases or other inquiries please contact:
harvest.equip@gmail.com

Endorsements for
DISCOVERING YOUR SPIRITUAL DNA

Discovering Your Spiritual DNA by Peter Wollensack is the most practical book I have ever read on this subject. Through the revelation in this book, you will discover how you best "fit" into your important function in the Body of Christ. It will help you to understand and better relate to others who see, react, respond and do things differently than you do. It will help you to step more fully into fulfilling your important, God-given destiny. I highly recommend this powerful, life-changing book. Once you have read it, you will be recommending it to all of your friends.

Dr. A.L. "Papa" Gill
International healing evangelist & teacher, Big Bear Lake, CA
—author with over 1 million books in print

After being in ministry for over 33 years, ministering in over 3,000 churches in 17 different countries, there is one common question that people ask me: "What is my place in the Body of Christ?" When you find your place the peace of God comes into your life. *Discovering Your Spiritual DNA* by Pastor Peter helps to answer this question. This book will also help pastors to better recognize the gifts that God has brought to their church to support his vision. Read this book and you will discover how to be all that God made you to be!

Dr. Buddy Bell
President and Founder of Ministry of Helps International
Tulsa, OK

This is an insightful and extraordinary book concerning the gifts God has given into the world. More than a few Christians are confused by what the Bible says about spiritual gifts in different passages of Scripture. Pastor Wollensack clears up any misunderstanding by showing how certain gifts originate from the Father, some from the Son and others from the Holy Spirit. After laying this critical foundation, the book then moves into an extremely practical section of gift discovery. This will help every believer to understand their function and place of service in the Body of Christ. I have come across many books over the years on gift discovery. This is one of the best I have found. It's an easy read, very practical and I highly recommend it.

Dr. Berin Gilfillan
Founder, ISOM & Good Shepherd Ministries, San Bernardino, CA
—ISOM has thousands of ministry training centers in 145 nations

Discovering Your Spiritual DNA will inspire you concerning the unique gifts and callings God has placed within you. It will help you find your true mission in life and accept yourself—your strengths and your weaknesses—so that you can maximize your potential, fulfill God's purposes for your life, and fit yourself into the body of Christ to advance God's kingdom. Understanding yourself, who you are, and who God has gifted you to be is one of the choicest discoveries of life. Let this marvelous book help you discover *your* spiritual DNA!

Dr. Mark Virkler
President & Founder,
Christian Leadership University, Cheektowaga, NY
—teaches internationally and has authored over 50 books

"A new approach! ...A simple approach! ...A challenging approach! ...A personalized approach!"

Pastor Peter's "approach" to the subject normally called "Motivational Gifts" is refreshing and one I believe will grab the attention of new believers and be beneficial to their spiritual growth in their discipleship walk. It will also benefit those older in their "walk with Christ" who have not discovered their "spiritual DNA" and will be motivated to expand their walk and ministry in their Church.

As an educator involved with multiple cultures, I see great potential for using this book as a text/workbook for "Gifts 101" and will be adding it to our curriculum. It is with anticipation I will watch to see the various languages in which it will be published.

Dr. David L. Deaton
Founder & President of Covenant Life University
Ft. Myers, FL
—CLU has overseas extensions/affiliate institutions in:
Ukraine, Russia, Israel (International Institute of Theology, Zoe)
Belgium (Logos Bible College)
Peru (Universidad Pacto de Vida)
Mexico (Rivers of Life Bible College).

What a refreshing and creative presentation of truth concerning who you are in Christ and what His gifts look like when expressed through His representatives! Pastor Peter, through *Discovering Your Spiritual DNA*, brings much needed light on the subject of spiritual gifts. Read. Embrace. Confidently use the gifts that Christ has given so that through you others are impacted in His name!

Bishop LaDonna Osborn, D. Min.
Founder and Overseer of the International Gospel Fellowship
CEO of Osborn Ministries International
Tulsa, OK
—Overseer of more than 700 churches in 35 nations

CONTENTS

PROLOGUE

"TOO LATE!"

J oin me for a few moments to imagine....

It is a bright and sunny summer day. Just a few wisps of white, puffy clouds are gracefully riding a gentle breeze across the deep blue sky. Slightly hunched, leaning on your time-trusted walking stick, you turn to gaze upward to take in as much of the wondrous beauty above as you can.

Filled with awe, you take a deep breath and nod, "Indeed, I've been *so* blessed. Jesus has made *all* the difference!"

Your enduring faith in Him has provided you with strength over the years. Despite all you've been through, you've even managed to live well past the "three-score and ten" years promised in Scripture.[1]

But where has all that time gone? It seems to have been so fleeting—ever more so with each passing year.

And now you find yourself acutely aware of the imminence of your "homecoming." Over the last few weeks, it is as if heaven has been beckoning you. The impression within has been unmistakable. And so today, you've spent hours perched on the veranda contemplating your past and "what might have been."

Whatever *did* happen to all those hopes and aspirations that were once so dear to your heart? It seems most of them disappeared as the years rolled by—like an overnight mist vaporized by the early morning sun. Yet, they were once so *real!* They were your *passion!*

You weathered the storms of life and managed to steer your course around the rocky shoals that destroyed so many others. But, still, there is a gnawing sense deep within that somehow those same storms ended up driving you far off course, that your true destination in life was meant to be different.

A nagging question sits like a heavy rock in your belly. It just won't go away. "Did I *really* do with my life what God had for me to do?"

You *really do* know the answer, of course. You tried your best to be "faithful to the end." But, somehow, *your* best wasn't enough. Somehow, some way, you *did* miss the mark. As you ponder these things, a voice within speaking no louder than a whisper confirms with an exclamation mark what you know to be true: "You *have* missed it!"

The time for excuses is long past. You wasted precious years going down roads that led to … nowhere. And along the way you even fell into a pitfall or two that the enemy of your soul designed to be your undoing.

Long ago it seemed so simple. You knew that God had a plan for your life. But somehow you were never quite able to find it. You were always so busy "living life." It was always one thing or another. And now it is too late.

"*Too late!*"— those words reverberate on the inside. And, so it seems, they will continue to resound until you take your final breath.

GETTING DIRECTIONS

Reflecting on wasted human potential, it can be observed that the greatest repositories of wealth in this world are not its bank vaults, gold or diamond mines, or oil fields—but its graveyards. The vast untapped potential that lies buried in them is incalculable.

Interred within are all the destinies never discovered, visions never pursued, and dreams never realized. Books unwritten, business ventures never begun, inventions never birthed, and careers that never got off the ground—all are lying "six feet under," lost forever.

Of course, our Maker planned it to be otherwise. He's the one who placed both the great potential and many dreams inside each of us. His purpose in doing so was that they would be realized and that He would be glorified.

Only by seeking Him and living intentionally can we even hope to fulfill the purpose and potential that lies within us. Learning from the Master, Jesus Christ, we are to pursue the wonderful adventure called life. That is the way He intended for us to live. But how many will even pause long enough to reflect on all He has given us, let alone take time to express gratitude? Far too few, to be sure. But let you be counted among those who do.

It's crazy. Jesus, the One whom many of us claim to be following, wants nothing more than to guide us through this mixed-up world in which we live. But it is clear that some are in far too much of a hurry, busily occupied with other things, to get His directions. It's like we are driving bleary-eyed toward God-only-knows where, speeding down the roadway of life, and won't slow down for a rest stop— let alone to ask for directions.

But it really doesn't take all that much to change things. It does require your s-l-o-w-i-n-g down and l-i-s-t-e-n-i-n-g. It also involves ditching a few wrong notions we have picked up along our journey through life.

But, since you are taking the time to read this book, it is clear that you are one of those who does have what it takes.

Notes

[1]See Psalm 90:10.

Chapter 1

BY DIVINE DESIGN

"Even before He made the world, God loved us and chose us in Christ...." (Ephesians 1:4, NLT)

IN HIS IMAGE

The God who spoke this world into existence[1] chose to make man, the crown of His creation, out of dust. Common... ordinary... dust.

The Lord's idea for this creature He was making, however, was far from ordinary, for the man, Adam, was to be made in image of the Creator Himself.

So, after forming the man, God (Yahweh) breathed into the man's nostrils and the man sprang to life.

Did you get that? The spark that brought Adam into existence was the very breath of the Living God!

From that point on the man and his companion, Eve, were "in tune" with their Maker. He had filled them with His Spirit. They fellowshipped with Him daily. They and their Creator walked and talked and enjoyed one other's company.

IN HARMONY

Scripture tells us that before God created man He spoke these words: "*Let us make man in our image and after our likeness.*"[2] The "us" the Lord was referring to was God the Father, God the Son, and God the Holy Spirit. So, in unison, the three-in-one Godhead created man. And the man and his mate were at "one" with the triune God.

Similar to the Godhead, Adam's and Eve's nature also had three parts— body, soul, and spirit. And because they were in tune with their Creator from the beginning, these three dimensions were also in harmony.

> *Adam had prodigious powers and wisdom to rule and reign on the earth that were contained in his "spiritual DNA."*

With his God-breathed spirit, Adam was capable of sensing the Lord's presence and communed with Him without hindrance. And this first man was given prodigious powers and wisdom to rule and reign on the earth. It was inherent within him—in his "spiritual DNA."

BEFORE CREATION

That was Adam in the beginning—but how is it with us?

As mind-boggling as it may seem, Scripture informs us that our heavenly Father knew each and every one of us even *before* Adam breathed his first breath! As hard as it may be for the human mind to grasp, we were on God's heart and mind even before the world began.[3]

But more than a few of us have fallen into the trap of thinking that we're not so special!

How's that?!? You are *indeed* special to the One who made you—so special in fact that He gave you distinctive gifts before you were even born!

And if that isn't enough to prove how valuable you are to Him, then this has to be the clincher: He willingly sent His Son to die on the cross at Calvary so that you can spend your eternity with Him!

As hard as it may be for us to comprehend, God had each one of us in His heart and mind even before the world began!

Notes

[1] See, for example, Genesis chapter 1:3, 6, 9.

[2] Genesis 1:26.

[3] *Even before He made the world, God loved us and chose us in Christ to be holy and without fault in His eyes.* (Ephesians 1:4, *NLT*)

Chapter 2

THE "GOD CODE" WITHIN

"For the invisible things of him... are clearly seen, being understood by the things that are made...." (Romans 1:20)

I n making you the one-of-a-kind person that you are, the Lord fashioned not only the physical "you"—your body— but the invisible "you"—your soul and spirit as well.

DNA—SPIRAL STRANDS OF LIFE

"...and knowledge shall be increased." (Daniel 12:4b)

A little more than a generation ago, scientists made an amazing discovery: All of the physical characteristics of a person—from the size and shape of his smile to the color of his hair— are encoded in a tiny spiral-shaped molecule called DNA, which is found within every cell in the human body.[1]

Though researchers are still far from understanding more than the basics of how DNA works, they do know this: Every detail about the development and functioning of a person's body exists in an incredibly complex genetic code contained in something so small that it is invisible to the naked eye. It is that tiny, and yet the amount of information contained within this molecule is said to be equal to that in a stack of eighty copies of the Bible.

> *Even though a DNA molecule is so tiny it can't be seen with the human eye, it contains as much information as a stack of 80 Bibles!*

As it is with many areas of human understanding, what scientists actually *know* about DNA is far less than the general public assumes they know. For example, until recently most researchers dismissed the bulk of the information "written" into the genetic code as merely "junk DNA"—that is, until it they discovered that it was in fact encrypted on a higher level than they had previously understood!

Experts are acutely aware that researchers must still discover much about DNA. They are beginning to investigate the profound implications of DNA's multi-level operations. Yet, long ago King David of Israel had a tremendous God-given insight into this very same matter. Writing about a revelation the Lord had given regarding the manner in which every person is fashioned, David marveled at how "remarkable" and "wonderfully complex" it all is.[2] Modern man is now just catching a glimpse of the many implications of such an astounding insight— revealed to David some 3,000 years ago.

ETERNITY WITHIN

"He has planted eternity in the human heart...."
(Ecclesiastes 3:11, NLT)

Indeed, the mechanism of DNA reflects our Creator's amazing ingenuity. It is all the more remarkable when we consider that our physical body is passing away and our sojourn in this world is fleeting because even a long life is but a passing moment.

Our soul and our spirit are of eternal significance. Is it even remotely possible that the One who has taken such great care in making each one of us as a unique individual has done any less in fashioning those two aspects of us that live forever? As noted earlier, we were in His heart and mind before He made the world. To be sure, He has carefully planned every facet of us—spirit, soul, and body. Nothing about us is accidental!

The sophistication we see in DNA is found throughout God's creation—from the inner workings of an atom to the vast reaches of the universe. We can observe patterns everywhere in the Lord's handiwork. What we can see in the visible realm reflects a purposeful design that also exists in a higher, spiritual dimension. In short, the operation of a DNA molecule in the physical world points to a similar reality in the invisible world—the realm of spiritual DNA.

SPIRITUAL DNA—WHAT IT IS AND WHAT IT IS NOT

According to this truth, let us clearly define what spiritual DNA is. Spiritual DNA is a unique combination of abilities and attributes that comprise a person's soul and spirit that the Lord gave to an individual before he or she was born for the purpose of glorifying God.

> *Spiritual DNA defined: It is a unique combination of abilities and attributes that comprise a person's soul and spirit that the Lord gave to an individual before he or she was born for the purpose of glorifying God.*

God has endowed every human being, without exception, with a spiritual DNA. That means that each and every one of us starts out in life as a debtor to Yahweh—whether he or she becomes an atheist, a New Ager, a Muslim, a secular humanist, a sun worshipper, or a born-again believer—because "it is He who has made us, and not we ourselves...."[3] The unbelieving world accepts myths such as the "self-made" man or woman. But, for the most part, we are what we are because of the way He made us to be.

It is important to keep in mind that God's intention in equipping a person with their distinctive spiritual DNA is not only that they would fulfill their purpose on earth but also that they will glorify Him. Spiritual DNA is not about "self-realization," as New Agers believe and teach—it *is* and always *will be* about *Him*.

While many New Age practitioners have taken the idea of spiritual DNA and added it to their amorphous and evolving belief system, the truth is that it is firmly rooted in Scripture. The notion of spiritual DNA is first seen "in the beginning" when God made man in His image and likeness—for when the Creator breathed life into Adam's nostrils He endowed him with a portion of His very own nature.

Although Adam and Eve were made perfect, having received their nature and attributes directly from God, after they fell into sin their offspring received only a portion of the original spiritual legacy. As with all the descendants of Adam, we receive much of our spiritual inheritance by means of our God-given spiritual DNA.

Some within the church, however, teach that spiritual DNA originates at the time of the New Birth. When they refer to "spiritual DNA," they have in mind the "new nature" given to a believer after the "old man" has passed away.[4] Other Christian teachers use the term "spiritual DNA" as a label for the fruit of the Spirit.[5]

Although both of these designations are metaphors that appear at first glance to have merit, in truth each has little that compares to the genetic code of physical DNA. Neither the new nature of man nor the fruit of the Spirit is connected to a one-of-a-kind, pre-determined, complex pattern within someone, like DNA. Both are related to the work of the Holy Spirit in a believer's life. While "putting on the new man" and growing in the fruit of the Spirit are essential to the *development* of a person's spiritual DNA, these and other uses of the term "spiritual DNA" are unfortunate because they obscure a more apt, deeper, biblical understanding.

SUMMING UP:

Physical DNA:

Is God's method of determining the physical characteristics of a person:

* It provides a "blueprint" for development.
* Provides detailed information (a genetic code) concerning the body.
* Every person has a distinctive DNA—no two people are alike.
* Scientists have a long way to go in unlocking many of the "secrets" of DNA.

Spiritual DNA:

Is a Bible-based concept about the soul and spirit of a person:

* It is analogous to physical DNA but operates in the invisible realm.
* Everyone has a unique spiritual DNA—no two people are alike.
* A person's spiritual DNA is a part of his or her inner being given by God before birth.
* It enables a person to fulfill his or her purpose in life and glorify the Lord.
* New Agers have tried to co-opt the idea of spiritual DNA and add it to their belief system.
* Some Christians have used the term "spiritual DNA" to signify the "new nature" of a person after being born again or as a label for the fruit of the Spirit.
  * These and other uses of the term are less appropriate and tend to cause confusion.

Notes

[1]DNA is an acronym for **d**eoxyribo**n**ucleic **a**cid. Not only humans, but every living organism—plant and animal—has the DNA molecule within every cell.

[2]See Psalm 139:14, HCSB and NLT.

[3]Psalm 100:3, NASB.

[4]See 2 Corinthians 5:17 and Ephesians 4:24.

[5]See Galatians 5:22-23.

Chapter 3

THE SEARCH BEGINS

"For in Him we live and move and have our being...."
(Acts 17:28, NKJV)

IT TAKES ALL KINDS

The famous Hollywood actor Marlon Brando when asked, "How are you?" once replied, "How do I know *how* I am, when I don't even know *who* I am?" His acerbic response to such a harmless question undoubtedly reflected a deep anguish within over not being able to see the meaning or significance of his life. Even though he had been successful from a worldly perspective, he was like so many others in failing miserably in what was more important—finding his true identity and purpose.

On the other hand, there are those fortunate few whose experience is astoundingly different. These are the rare souls who from an early age are sure of what they want to do and what it is they want out of life. They are the children who can answer the question "What do you want to be when you grow up?" directly and without hesitation.

No matter how successful a person becomes in the world's eyes, if he hasn't discovered his true identity and purpose he has failed in God's eyes.

I remember a classmate of mine who in his early teen years wanted to become a doctor. From the way he applied himself in school and arranged his priorities it was obvious that he was pretty serious about it. Having lost contact with him since those school years several decades ago, I recently checked to see what had become of him. Well, sure enough, he became a neurosurgeon and has maintained a successful medical practice in New York City for more than 35 years.

How simple it is for some people—or so it seems.

WHERE TO START?

There was a popular song in the early 1980s that had the catchy title of *Looking for Love in all the Wrong Places*. It seems that when it comes to searching for purpose in their life, most people are doing the same thing—looking for it in all the wrong places.

So, let's avoid making the same mistake and be more efficient in our search. To do so, let us recall a few of the observations already made. We understand that:

- God knew about each one of us long before we were born.
- He has given us special gifts and abilities.
- Our spiritual DNA makes us what we are on the inside—in our soul and spirit. It contains all of the qualities that make each of us unique, distinctive.

Furthermore, we also understand from the Scriptures that the Lord is not whimsical—He is a God of purpose who has an end in mind before He even begins.[1] To be sure, Yahweh made us with a spiritual

DNA that is connected with the purpose for which He has made us.

To discover our spiritual DNA, it only makes good sense to consult with the One who has made us. That is where our search begins.

> *Our loving Father has fashioned our soul and spirit with a spiritual DNA that is connected with the purpose for which He has made us.*

A WORD TO THE WISE

"Oh, the depth of the riches both of the wisdom and knowledge of God!" (Romans 11:33, NASB)

Fortunately our Maker hasn't left us here in this world as orphans on our own. The incredible truth is that He has given us every provision we need for our stay here on earth and has provided us with a trusty guidebook as well. To those who have received His Son as their Lord and Savior, He has provided a steady and sure compass to keep us right on track in our journey through life—His Holy Spirit.

The Word of God—the Holy Bible—is our instruction manual. It is far more, however. It is a storehouse of insight and understanding—a veritable repository containing the wisdom of the Ages.

There is no need for us to follow the rabbit trails others have left. In the end, pursuits that are not God-ordained will prove to be pointless and futile.

With the Holy Spirit guiding us, let us discover the purpose for which our Creator made us by looking in the Word of God.

Let us begin now, for destiny is calling!

Notes

[1] See Hebrews 13:8 and Isaiah 46:10.

Chapter 4

GRACED BY GOD

SUPERNATURALLY ENDOWED

"God's gifts of grace come in many forms...."
(1 Peter 4:10a, NIRV)

The God who is Spirit has *supernaturally* placed a particular spiritual DNA inside of each one of us. The various aspects of that gift can be considered as "graces"—abilities and aptitudes that are from God Himself. They originate in the invisible dimension of the soul and spirit. In other words, they reside in eternity—outside the realm of the flesh.

Your spiritual DNA is supernatural because your supernatural God has endowed you with it!

We can catch a small glimpse of this reality in what the Lord said to the prophet Jeremiah when He called him to serve as a prophet:

Before I formed you in the womb I knew you, before you were born
I set you apart; I appointed you as a prophet to the nations.[1]

Yahweh fashioned the spirit and soul of Jeremiah in such a way that
he would be able to fulfill his God-ordained destiny on this earth. And,
He has done the same thing for each of us as well.

GRACE PACKAGES

While every person has a distinctive combination of traits and abilities, Scripture provides a clear idea as to the general categories or types
of "grace packages" with which He endows the sons and daughters of
Adam. These are revealed to us in Romans 12:6-8[2]:

Having then gifts differing according to the grace that is given to
*us, let us use them: if **prophecy**, let us prophesy in proportion to*
*our faith; or **ministry**, let us use it in our ministering; he who*
***teaches**, in teaching; he who **exhorts**, in exhortation; he who*
***gives**, with liberality; he who **leads**, with diligence; he who shows*
***mercy**, with cheerfulness.*

These verses mention seven endowments[3]:

- Prophecy
- Ministry(Serving)
- Teaching
- Exhorting (Encouraging)
- Giving (Sharing)
- Leading (Administration)
- Mercy (Compassion)

In reality, each of these gifts represents a category of spiritual
DNA that has a variety of characteristics. Once we arrive at a spiritual

understanding of the attributes of each grace package, it will become clear that these are truly *supernatural* endowments and not merely character traits or natural abilities.

THE PAGAN DECEPTION

"And do not be conformed to this world, but be transformed by the renewing of your mind, that you may prove what is that good and acceptable and perfect will of God." (Romans 12:2, NKJV)

Contemporary society's ideas about personality traits are derived mainly from theories developed long ago. People in ancient times before the days Jesus Christ walked the face of the earth recognized different types of human temperament and developed a theoretical scheme. Hippocrates, known as the "father of western medicine," was a physician who lived in Greece four centuries before Christ and is credited with developing the first system of classifying what he theorized are four basic kinds of personality.[4]

This system of "four human temperaments" was widely accepted throughout the western world until the second half of the twentieth century. As Christians, however, we need to consider that Hippocrates was a *pagan* physician whose insight was not given to him by God—he was limited to his own natural understanding and his theory in no way reflects godly, spiritual insight.

Although it may seem ludicrous to us now, Hippocrates' theory was based upon the notion that there are four different kinds of fluids in the body, which he called "humors," that determine human temperament. Remarkably, though this part of his theory has been totally discredited, the influence of the other part—of the "four personality types"—still lingers until this day.

Though modern psychology has modified the classification of temperament somewhat, current psychological schemes are still based solely on sense knowledge and to an extent derived from Hippocrates' observations. As such, they merely represent a feeble attempt to explain why people "are the way they are" without the benefit of the light of Scripture or the input of the One who has made us.

Why do Christians believe more in the disproven theories about human personality concocted by a pagan Greek physician than what their Bible has to say about such matters?

The question is: Why, then, do so many who think of themselves as Bible-believing Christians—who supposedly "put the Word first" in their lives—base their concepts about personality on secular psychology whose ideas originated in ancient, pagan Greece? It should not be so!

How much better it is for the people of God to discover what the *Scriptures* have to say about such matters concerning the soul and spirit and break free from natural, sense-based understanding. Let us renew our minds with the Word of God and arrive at a spiritual, godly understanding.

Notes

[1] Jeremiah 1:5, NIV.

[2] NKJV.

[3] Alternative names for these gifts are shown in parentheses. These, as well as other names are used in other translations.

[4] These four basic types of human temperament are sanguine, phlegmatic, choleric, and melancholic.

Chapter 5

THREE SETS OF GIFTS

"Now about the spiritual gifts (the special endowments of super-natural energy), brethren, I do not want you to be misinformed." (1 Corinthians 12:1, AMP)

TOTALLY SUPERNATURAL

To continue our investigation into discovering our spiritual DNA we must clearly establish a few simple concepts concerning the types of gifts mentioned in the New Testament. We do this because once we understand that there are three distinct *kinds* of gifts, each with a *different* nature and purpose, the gifts that are part of a person's spiritual DNA will become more obvious.

To gain deeper insight, we need to start with the basic premise that it is God who is *Spirit* who has provided all of the gifts. Since this is true, *all* of the gifts are spiritual in nature. In fact, they are all *supernatural* because they come from our supernatural God.

Therefore, no set of gifts is more "spiritual" than another and no set of gifts is more "supernatural" than another.

The three sets of gifts in the New Testament are listed in:

> *All of the gifts are spiritual in nature—in fact, they are all supernatural. One set of gifts is not more "spiritual" or more "supernatural" than another.*

* Romans 12:6-8
* Ephesians 4:11-12
* 1 Corinthians 12:8-10

The Scriptures mention a number of other gifts, but for our understanding we will focus on these three sets of gifts that figure so prominently in the New Testament. Perhaps you are already somewhat familiar with these groups of gifts.

* We mentioned the first set, listed in Romans 12:6-8, in the previous chapter. Most often commentators refer to them as the "motivational gifts," but that name is inadequate because each gift involves many attributes, or graces, that God deposits within a person before birth and that are manifested in a variety of ways. In other words, these gifts contain abilities and spiritual qualities that involve far more than a person's motivation. Since God bestows every one of these gifts for His purpose, a more appropriate name for them is the "endowment gifts," which is the term we will use.
* The second set of gifts, listed in Ephesians 4:11-12, is sometimes called the "ministry gifts" or the "five-fold ministry gifts." Since each of the gifts in this set has the purpose of equipping the saints to do the work of the ministry, the more apt name for them is the "equipping gifts," which is the term we will use for them.
* The third set of gifts, listed in 1 Corinthians 12:8-10, is some-

times called the "gifts of the Holy Spirit" or the "spiritual gifts." While it is true that they come from the Holy Spirit; they are operations or manifestations of the Spirit that meet a particular need at a specific time. And since all three of the gift categories are spiritual in nature, a more appropriate name for this set of gifts is the "manifestation gifts," which is the term we will use for them.

So, the three sets of gifts are the endowment gifts, the equipping gifts, and the manifestation gifts. Within these three categories, there are 21 gifts in all, as indicated in the table below.

The Three Sets of Gifts		
Endowment Gifts (7)	Equipping Gifts (5)	Manifestation Gifts (9)
Romans 12:6-8	Ephesians 4:11-12	1 Corinthians 12:8-10
prophet server teacher exhorter giver leader mercy giver	apostle prophet evangelist pastor teacher[1]	*Speaking Gifts:* • tongues • interpretation of tongues • prophecy *Power Gifts:* • faith • gifts of healing • miracles *Revelation Gifts:* • discerning of spirits • word of wisdom • word of knowledge

The important thing to remember is that while an endowment gift is *innate* within an individual, an equipping gift is a *person* who has been chosen by Jesus Christ as a gift to His Body, and a manifestation gift is an *operation* of the Holy Spirit at a point in time to meet a need.

THREE GIVERS AND THREE PURPOSES

The key to understanding the difference between each of these sets is knowing the purpose for which they are given and also by whom.

The giver of the endowment gifts is the Father, our Creator, so that a person can fulfill his destiny or "mission" in life. A person doesn't just "happen" to have certain attributes—the Father placed them inside the individual before birth so that he could accomplish his God-given purpose. Every person born in this world has been given a least one primary endowment gift.

The giver of the equipping gifts is the Son who gives them to the church. An equipping gift is a *person* who is called by Jesus Christ to serve as a leader for the purpose of equipping the body of Christ for service. Whether a person is an apostle, prophet, evangelist, pastor, or teacher, he has been chosen—appointed and anointed—by Jesus Christ Himself for training the saints to do the work of the ministry.[2]

The Holy Spirit gives the manifestation gifts to meet the needs of people. Each gift operates through a believer who makes himself or herself available for service. The believer who functions in a Holy Spirit gifting doesn't *own* the gift but rather is a *vessel* through which the gift manifests. The purpose of the gift is to fulfill a need such as healing, giving a word of knowledge, or any other of the nine manifestations of the Holy Spirit.

To summarize, God the Father has given at least one the seven endowment gifts to all persons alive, whether they have come into a saving knowledge of Him or not; God the Son has given five equipping gifts to His church so that it grows toward maturity and comes into the full measure of "the stature of Christ"; and God the Holy Spirit operates through Spirit-filled believers by means of nine manifestation gifts to meet specific needs as He wills.

These key points are summarized in the chart below.

Our Triune God and His Three Sets of Gifts[3]		
The Giver	Father	Son	Holy Spirit
The Gift	Endowment Gifts	Equipping Gifts	Manifestation Gifts
Given To	All Mankind	The Church	Meet Particular Needs

WHAT'S IN A NAME?

One possible area of confusion arises from the fact that both the endowment and the equipping gift sets have within them a teaching gift and a prophetic gift. Although these gifts have the same name, it is clear they are not one and the same gift because the respective groups they are in have different functions and purposes.

To clarify the matter, we need to consider that oftentimes a word can have a number of meanings that depend on the context in which the word is used. Multiple meanings for a single word occur in every language, including Greek, the language in which the New Testament was written.[4]

The *endowment gift* teacher has an array of characteristics and abilities that are innate within all persons with the gift, regardless of whether they are engaged in teaching as a vocation or not. This gifting is an integral part of their spiritual DNA and manifests through their personality and abilities. An *equipping gift* teacher is someone who has been called and anointed to teach the body of Christ. Such a person may have any one of the seven endowment giftings—and the qualities that go along with it—but the key point is that the person has been chosen by Jesus Christ to equip the saints for service.

It is likewise with the prophetic gift. The *endowment gift* prophet has certain personality traits and aptitudes that were placed inside him before he was born. This person may or may not function within the church as a recognized prophet. On the other hand, an *equipping gift* prophet is someone Jesus Christ has appointed to provide spiritual discernment and direction as a prophetic spokesman to the body of Christ.

Notes

[1] The gifts of pastor and teacher are referred to in the original Greek manuscripts in a way that indicates that pastor and teacher are interrelated gifts and are (perhaps) one gift—that is, "pastor-teacher."

[2] Unfortunately, many Bible-believing groups do not recognize or acknowledge the validity of all of the equipping gifts. Therefore, any person who is convinced that Jesus has called him and bestowed upon him an equipping gift is responsible to the One who has called him and must look for a local church where his equipping gift is recognized and appreciated.

[3] Another "witness" or confirmation of the truths in this table is found in 1 Corinthians 12 where the apostle Paul referred to "varieties of **gifts**" (the word is "*charisma*" in Greek) in verse 4, "varieties of **ministries**" ("*diakonia*") in verse 5, and "varieties of **effects**" ("*energema*") in verse 6. These should be understood as sub-categories of the spiritual or supernatural "*pneumatikos*" that he started to explain in verse 1 of the same chapter.

- The gifts ("*charisma*," or plural "*charismata*") Paul referred to in verse 4 are "spiritual endowments" according to *Strong's Concordance*. They parallel the gifts ("*charisma*") he wrote about in Romans 12:6-8, the **endowment gifts**, which are **given by the Father**.
- The ministries, or "*diakonia*," Paul referred to also carry the sense of "service" or "office," again according to *Strong's Concordance*. These correspond, therefore, to the **equipping gifts** (or five-fold ministry gifts), the "*doma*" referred to in Ephesians 4:8, that are listed in Ephesians 4:11, and are **given by the Son**.
- The "effects," or "*energema*," can also be understood as "operations" or "workings" according to Strong. These are also referred to as manifestations ("*phanerosis*") in verse 8 of first Corinthians. Clearly, these are the **manifestation gifts** listed in 1 Corinthians 12:8-10 which are **given by the Holy Spirit**.

In sum, by combining the insight gained from all of these verses, we see that the gifts ("*charismata*") are from the Father, ministries ("*diakonia*") are from the Son and effects ("*energema*") or manifestations ("*phanerosis*") are from the Holy Spirit.

While each of the three supernatural categories of what the apostle Paul calls "spirituals" ("*pneumatikos*") are distinct, it should be recognized that there also is a degree of interrelatedness among them. At the very least, the Giver in each case is part of the tri-unity of the Godhead and in a very real sense each one represents an aspect or facet of God's love.

[4] In English, for example, the word "rose" can refer to a beautiful, fragrant flower or be the past tense of the word rise, which means to move upward. Another example is the word "stalk" which can refer either to apart of a plant or to following or harassing a person.

Chapter 6

STEPPING BEYOND THE THRESHOLD

YOUR SPIRITUAL DNA AFFECTS EVERYTHING

Each of the seven endowment gifts (*"charismata"*) referred to in Romans 12:6-8 is in reality a "grace package" that has a *set* of attributes. These traits constitute the most prominent part of your spiritual DNA. Some of the qualities of your endowment gifting became obvious in the early years of your life, manifesting primarily as the personality traits that were obvious to those around you, whereas other attributes become more pronounced as you matured.

The "way you are"—your temperament, ways of thinking, demeanor, attitudes, abilities, and predispositions—has been determined mainly by the spiritual DNA that your Creator placed within before you were born. There are other factors involved as well, however—such as your life experiences, the cultural

> *Our spiritual DNA is perhaps the single biggest factor in determining how someone looks at, reacts to, and functions in life.*

and social environment in which you were raised, and the education and training you've received, as well as the of level of spiritual maturity you've attained. All of these factors combine to make you the person you are and to a large degree determine how you look at, react to, and function in the world around you.

Few of us appreciate just how much of "who we are" is determined by what God placed within us before we were born. Consider the fact that a person's spiritual DNA causes him or her to:

* look at every life situation and relationship from a particular frame of reference
* act according to certain patterns of behavior
* be motivated in ways according to his or her gifting

It is as if the spiritual DNA with which every one of us is born functions as a pair of tinted glasses that have the particular "color" of our gifting. The "tint" of their gifting affects their perceptions of everything around them, as well as their reaction to it.

ACTIVATING YOUR FULL POTENTIAL

Nearly everyone has latent potential within—a portion of the spiritual DNA that is dormant— but that is yet to become manifest. The key to unlocking that potential is attaining a certain level of spiritual maturity, a threshold, at which point the unrealized quality or ability can be "activated." That threshold is as distinctive as a person's endowment gifting, and stepping across it depends on when or whether he arrives at that point in his spiritual journey through life.

From a biblical perspective, the basic requirement for all spiritual development in God's kingdom is that a person first be "born again" into His family.[1] Once that supernatural occurrence has taken place, a person then undergoes a spiritual process whereby his "inner man" develops to become more in line with his Maker's original intent. That spiritual journey is fostered by meditating on the Word of God and abiding in the True Vine. As a person grows and is transformed, he becomes more and more like Jesus Christ.

At some point along the way, special abilities and anointings that are part of the person's spiritual DNA—ones that have been latent— will spring to life and become operational. These distinctive aspects of the person's grace package become a more significant force, enabling him to walk more fully in the totality of his spiritual gifting.

For the sake of simplicity and clarity, the description of each grace package in the next seven chapters focuses primarily on the positive characteristics of the gift package—that is, "what it looks like" when developed in a healthy manner. When a person is attuned to God's heart and manifests the fruit of the Spirit in his life, he will also be able to walk in the strength and fullness of his gifting.

We should note, however, that each gift has a "downside" as well that results from a failure to develop spiritually and walk in the God-kind of love. In reality, everyone is at a different point along the road to spiritual maturity—some more developed and some less.

There is an interesting parallel to this in the physical world. Scientists have discovered that a person's attitude and words can have a dramatic effect on the physical DNA within his body.[2] A positive, loving attitude and kind words have been proven to cause positive changes in a person's physical DNA that result in a beneficial effect on physical health and well-being. On the other hand, negative emotions and attitudes have a detrimental effect on the molecular structure of the physical DNA, which adversely impacts a person's health and well-being. In other words, scientists have corroborated the biblical truth that "*A cheerful heart is good medicine, but a broken spirit saps a person's strength.*"[3]

> *When you are attuned to God's heart and manifest the fruit of the Spirit in your life, you will also be able to walk in the strength and fullness of your gifting.*

Self-centeredness, carnality, strongholds in the mind, and worldliness are all enemies of developing in your spiritual DNA as God intended.

If you are a person who is beset by any of these shortcomings and are not able to overcome them, you will never be able to develop your God-given abilities to full maturity, and the potential of your spiritual DNA will remain mostly unfulfilled. What a tragedy that would be!

Notes

[1] See John 3:16.

[2] These test results are reported in the article "You can Change Your DNA," dated 7/9/12, from the Institute of HeartMath website (*www.heartmath.org*). Other DNA experiments have demonstrated similar results.

[3] Proverbs 17:22, *NLT*.

Chapter 7

THE SPIRITUAL DNA OF AN ENDOWMENT GIFT PROPHET

"...for the testimony of Jesus is the spirit of prophecy."
(Revelation 19:10)

Those whose spiritual DNA demonstrates the pattern of an endowment gift prophet have at the core of their being an exceptional ability to discern spiritual matters and a spiritual "radar" to detect issues of the heart.

Such persons are not only enabled to perceive things that others fail to recognize, but their grace package also gives them the ability to verbalize that which they have seen in a clear and concise manner. In fact, because of their verbal skills and understanding of human nature they tend to be persuasive if they are mature in their gifting.

If you are an endowment gift prophet, you will have a strongly developed sense of right and wrong and, therefore, are not the kind of person who is typically willing to "go along to get along." In fact, in a group setting you will usually be more candid and forthright than others and for this reason you may at times be perceived as a malcontent or misfit because of your outspokenness and opposition to compromise what you believe is right. If you are a Christian with this gifting, your attitude and behavior are based on a firm belief that for a person to observe or discern sin and say nothing is in and of itself a sin.

A basic motivation of a person with the spiritual makeup of an endowment gift prophet is the need to categorize everything in a clearly defined way—with no fuzzy edges or shades of gray. As such, if you are a prophet you will tend to see things in terms of "black or white," "right or wrong," "good or bad," and "true or false." Because of this predisposition, you may sometimes seem rigid and inflexible to others.

If someone with this gift is not careful to operate in love and with wisdom, the tendency to be uncompromising and outspoken will cause friction with others perhaps to the point of rupturing relationships. I have known more than a few with this gifting who have had great difficulty keeping a job for any length of time or maintaining long-lasting friendships.

The good news is that if you have this bundle of God-given abilities, in a church setting you are the one who will function as a "canary in a coal mine" when it comes to sin. Because you are constantly alert to the spiritual atmosphere in any group environment, you will almost always be the first to sense when sin is seeking to insinuate itself into a ministry.

Many who have a prophetic grace package will also tend to be the first to speak out about injustice or unequal treatment caused by double standards. This spiritual DNA configuration will also cause them to be particularly sensitive to hypocrisy when those in leadership display it and typically will not remain silent when someone in that position is insincere or shows double standards.

One of the most prominent features of the spiritual makeup of endowment gift prophets is that they exhibit more of a vertical orientation than a horizontal one. What this means is that someone with this endowment will be more preoccupied with motivations and actions that could cause them to be alienated from God than they are concerned with whether they become estranged from those around them. Their motto is "In God I trust," and they are willing to let the consequences of that trust rest in His hands—come what may.

An endowment gift prophet's primary orientation is vertical rather than horizontal.

If you have been endowed with the grace package of a prophet and are a born-again believer, you will tend to stand out in comparison with others by your concern for having a clear conscience before God. This concern is rooted in another issue that is important to you—the high value you place on truth.

One of the exceptional qualities of a person with the endowment gift prophet's spiritual DNA is that he[1] tends to be more teachable than others, particularly when discipline or correction is required. He is also usually more open about personal sin than most people who typically prefer to conceal their wrong attitudes and transgressions. Others may want to "look good," but to the prophet it is far more important to "be good" and to set things right.

The Apostle Peter is a wonderful example of an endowment gift prophet in the Scriptures. For instance, of the 12 disciples, Peter was the first to discern and profess the profound truth that Jesus is "… *the Messiah, the Son of the living God.*"[2] He also displayed tremendous spiritual insight and persuasive ability, both of which are characteristics of an endowment gift prophet, when he preached his first sermon on the day of Pentecost. In his message he tied together spiritual truths from the Scriptures, truths that had been hidden from mankind until that day, and preached such a compelling message that within a matter of a few days the church grew to several thousand believers.

Peter also demonstrated his prophetic gift in his outspokenness without regard for the consequences. He displayed this kind of courage on several occasions, such as when he boldly confronted the ruling council of Jews, the Sanhedrin, charging them with the responsibility of having put the Messiah to death. Though his brave actions could easily have cost him his life, he refused to let them cow him because speaking the truth was much more important than whatever might happen to him.

Peter was also notable for his impetuosity, which is another inherent quality of an endowment gift prophet. He frequently responded to situations on impulse—such as when he climbed over the side of the boat to walk on water at Jesus' invitation and also when he lopped off the ear of the high priest's servant on the night of Jesus' arrest.

A few of the main strengths of the spiritual DNA of an endowment gift prophet are that they:

1. have a keen sense of right and wrong
2. can discern others' motives and character
3. are candid and persuasive
4. see things in "black and white" and not shades of gray
5. have strict personal standards and tend to be hard on themselves
6. are loyal to truth rather than to people
7. are intolerant of hidden sin and hypocrisy
8. are more teachable than others when discipline or correction is needed

A few of the weaknesses of this gifting are a tendency to:

1. be insensitive to others' feelings since they are not people-pleasers
2. judge too quickly or too harshly
3. intimidate or offend others with bluntness and outspokenness
4. react harshly to sinners and cut off people who fail
5. struggle with self-image problems
6. be negative or gloomy in their approach to life because of their deep awareness of sin
7. be impulsive and compulsive
8. be hindered in close relationships

HOW MUCH OF AN ENDOWMENT GIFT PROPHET ARE YOU?

In order to understand more about your spiritual DNA, you will need to rate yourself as to how much you identify with being an endowment gift prophet.

So, on a scale of 0 to 4—with 0 meaning "not at all like me" and 4 meaning "that's just like me"— respond to the following statements. Write the appropriate number in the box next to each statement and then add up your score from each statement in the box at the bottom.

Remember

0 means "**not at all** like me"
1 means "**slightly** like me"
2 means "**somewhat** like me"
3 means "**mostly** like me"
4 means "**very much** like me"

---

1. I tend to be more alert to hidden motives and dishonesty than most people.

2. Many times I feel compelled to speak up to defend the truth or what is right.

3. Oftentimes I feel a responsibility to correct those who do wrong.

4. When it comes to speaking the truth, I do so in a direct manner. I am not the type to be overly diplomatic or "beat around the bush" with people.

5. Oftentimes I will form opinions and make judgments quickly.

☐ 6. I am willing to speak out for the truth even if it is unpopular and brings ridicule or antagonism against me.

☐ 7. Since I have a keen sense of right and wrong, I tend to see situations in terms of black and white and not in shades of gray.

☐ 8. I tend to be open about my own faults with others.

☐ 9. I am more loyal to truth than I am to people.

☐ 10. Because of my strict standards and frankness I have not had many close friendships in my life.

☐ 11. I feel uncomfortable around those who sin without repenting and changing. I try to distance myself from people like this.

☐ 12. I am more serious about the things of God than other people are and am introspective by nature.

☐ **TOTAL SCORE: ENDOWMENT GIFT PROPHET**

Notes

[1]Throughout the text, to avoid the repetitive use of "he and she" or "his and her," the terms "he" or "his" are used. However, unless referring to a particular individual, the masculine form is not to be taken as being gender specific and, therefore, denotes a person of either gender.
[2]Matthew 16:16, NLT.

Chapter 8

THE SPIRITUAL DNA OF A SERVER (MINISTER)

"If God has been generous with you, he will expect you to serve him well. But if he has been more than generous, he will expect you to serve him even better." (Luke 12:48, CEV)

One of the key components of the serving gift, also known as the ministry gift, is the ability to readily discern practical needs that other people oftentimes fail to see. The other aspect of this inherent trait is that once a serving-gifted person becomes aware of a need, he or she will typically feel an impulse to do promptly whatever it takes to meet the need.

Persons endowed with this gift are most attracted to those tasks they can take care of in a short amount of time. In general, endowment gift ministers will have little interest in any project that has the possibility of becoming a long, drawn-out venture. If servers do happen to become involved in an undertaking that becomes bogged down, showing little apparent progress over time, it is likely that their frustration level will increase accordingly.

If you are ministry-gifted, you almost certainly will be the kind of person who feels that the best way for you to show love is through deeds and actions rather than by words only. You will also be the type to find great satisfaction and even joy just doing things of a practical nature that are helpful to those around you whom you care about.

If you are a server, your spiritual DNA will also cause you to be alert to the special interests of people around you. A related trait in this gift package is that you are not only skilled at finding out others' preferences but also have a distinct ability to remember their likes and dislikes.

> *A ministry-gifted person feels that the best way to show love is through deeds and actions rather than by words only.*

A basic feature of the spiritual makeup of the ministry gift is for a server to be straightforward and honest. If such persons are mature in their gifting, they will be guileless and can be entrusted with responsibilities. Those being helped do not have to be overly concerned about the server's loyalty or being taken advantage of or defrauded.

When helping someone, those with a ministry gifting normally want clear instructions and direction before beginning the task at hand. Since servers consider those they are assisting as being in the lead role, and desire to please that person, they are uncomfortable having to second-guess them—particularly if the minister isn't familiar with the person's way of doing things.

Those endowed with the spiritual DNA of a server also need to feel appreciated. They often end up being the unsung heroes on a project, especially since they typically work behind the scenes. Those in charge often take the server's contribution for granted or overlook them, causing the server to feel slighted, especially because they are aware that their contribution is vital to the successful completion of the project.

Since ministry-gifted persons have an inner desire to help, they sometimes find it difficult to say "no" to people who request their assistance. The result, if they are not careful, is that their schedule can become overly hectic to the detriment of their more important responsibilities.

In some cases, this can cause the server's spiritual life to suffer or harm the family through neglect due to the server's misplaced priorities. This latter danger is ironic because most servers' tendency is to be highly protective of their family.

Those endowed with the server grace package need to use wisdom to prevent themselves from being exploited by those who may try to manipulate them because of their good-natured willingness to help out.

A Christian believer with this gift who is spiritually attuned will typically go above and beyond what is expected of them not only for the sake of the person being served but also because whatever they do is done "*heartily, as unto the Lord, and not unto men.*"[1] A typical server is disposed to "go the second mile," and others can depend on them even when the going gets rough.

Jesus Christ provides a perfect portrait of a serving-gifted person. He was down-to-earth and practical, trained as a youth to work with His hands—learning the practical skills of the carpentry trade from His step-father Joseph. During the years of His ministry, He was always at home with the common folk, and when He taught them He drew His examples and parables from the common everyday experiences of their lives.

There was nothing flamboyant about Him because His desire was to please His heavenly Father and not draw undue attention to Himself. Even though signs and wonders followed Him continually, on more than a few occasions He told the people who received a miracle at His hands to tell no one about it. Though He certainly was at the center of attention throughout His public ministry, He at no time sought the limelight.

One sure sign of the ministry gifting is a desire to live in a simple and uncomplicated way. Jesus lived humbly, being about His heavenly Father's business at all times, and modeled such a simple lifestyle that He was able to say, "*The foxes have holes and birds of the air have nests, but the Son of Man has nowhere to lay His head.*"[2]

Throughout His ministry, Jesus taught that the way to greatness is through service to others. In the Upper Room, on the last night He was with the Twelve, He demonstrated in a startling way what the heart of service is all about by washing His disciples' feet—all 24 feet (!)—including those of the one who would betray Him later that night. In doing this, Jesus humbly took on a task performed only by the lowliest of servants—washing away the dirt and grime from the day's comings and goings on the dusty streets of Jerusalem.

A few of the main strengths of those with the spiritual DNA of a minister or server are that they:

1. have a heart for "doing"
2. are quick to see and meet practical needs
3. like short-range projects
4. don't like being in the spotlight—like playing "second fiddle"
5. need to feel appreciated
6. have less difficulty with obedience than those with other gifts
7. desire to have and work best when there is clear direction
8. show love for others in deeds and actions more than through words

A few of the weaknesses of this gifting are a tendency to:

1. be critical with others when they don't help out with obvious needs
2. be exploited by others who take advantage of their willingness to serve
3. fail to delegate responsibilities since they prefer to do it themselves
4. become too pushy or interfering in their eagerness to help out
5. be easily hurt when they feel unappreciated
6. be overly protective of family members when a threat is perceived
7. become overextended in their commitments and let their schedule get out of control
8. become frustrated with long-term projects and goals

HOW MUCH OF A MINISTER OR SERVER ARE YOU?

Please rate yourself as to how much you identify with being an endowment gift minister.

As you did in the previous chapter, respond to the following statements as they apply to you by filling in each box with a number from 0 to 4. Write the appropriate number in the box next to each statement and then add up your score from each statement in the box at the bottom.

> ### Remember
>
> 0 means "**not at all** like me"
> 1 means "**slightly** like me"
> 2 means "**somewhat** like me"
> 3 means "**mostly** like me"
> 4 means "**very much** like me"

[ ] 1. I am usually neat, well organized, and detailed.

[ ] 2. I tend to be a very helpful person.

[ ] 3. I work better when there are only a few things to do and they are specific projects.

[ ] 4. I notice when things need to be done and jump in to help.

[ ] 5. I have a hard time saying no to requests for help.

[ ] 6. I prefer short-term projects over long-term projects.

[ ] 7. I usually prefer to do work myself rather than delegate it.

[ ] 8. I'd rather show others I love them by doing something for them. Actions speak.

☐   9.   I need to feel useful and appreciated.

☐   10. I get a lot of joy out of knowing that I'm being helpful.

☐   11. I'm not usually a leader, but I like to assist and support those in leadership.

☐   12. I enjoy working in a group, especially if there is a leader, the project is organized, and there are clear instructions.

☐   **TOTAL SCORE: SERVER**

Notes

[1]See Colossians 3:23.
[2]Matthew 8:20, NKJV.

Chapter 9

THE SPIRITUAL DNA OF AN ENDOWMENT GIFT TEACHER

"The large crowd enjoyed listening to Jesus teach."
(Mark 12:37, CEV)

One of the distinguishing marks of the spiritual makeup of an endowment gift teacher is an abiding thirst for truth. The effect of this God-given, inner drive is that a person with this grace package is motivated to go beyond what is obvious in dealing with the issues of life in order to ferret out the heart of a matter and "get to the bottom of things."

Another distinguishing mark of this gift is a predisposition and attributes that equip a person to assess the facts of any given situation and systematically sift through the details in order to arrive at a greater level of understanding in determining the truth. This trait, as well as their thoroughness, makes a spiritually developed endowment gift teacher a veritable "truth detective."

If you are an endowment gift teacher, your approach to issues or circumstances will typically be to look at it from a logical perspective, wanting to separate fact from fiction and determine the root causes of a problem. In addition, your basic attitude will be that truth has an inherent power within itself to set people free from superstition and spiritual bondage and to make situations right. Your ability to explain things is what makes all of this possible.

These traits within the spiritual DNA of the teaching gift are the perfect antidote whenever people are being led astray by fuzzy thinking, sentimentality, or subjectivity. After all, there is a deceiver who is continually seeking to steer God's people down the wrong road—one that will end up causing them great harm. Because of that, spiritually mature teachers are indispensable for protecting the church from error and apostasy. Such a teacher will serve in the role of a watchman—one who not only spots dangerous trends, influences, and teachings but also exposes them by speaking out and sharing his insight.

> *Concern for truth makes endowment gift teachers veritable "truth detectives."*

Because the endowment gift teachers' inclination is to "weigh matters" before speaking—carefully considering all of the aspects of an issue—they will seldom be the first to speak out, especially in a group discussion. Their preference is to hold their thoughts until they become convinced that the insight they possess is crucial to bring before the meeting—particularly when the group needs to make a decision. The reason for their reluctance to speak out earlier is that a teacher is the one most aware that all factors need to be considered without bias to arrive at a proper decision. Teachers view their role as the one who brings further clarity and balance to the discussion, especially if it is going in the wrong direction or isn't considering all of the pertinent facts.

Related to this is that teachers tend to look at things "philosophically," meaning that they usually evaluate problems and situations by placing them in the overall context more than others would. For this reason, they tend to be less emotional in reacting to either negative or positive situations and sometimes take things less "personally" than others.

A person with the grace package of a teacher also tends to be non-confrontational in his style, particularly compared to an endowment gift prophet. For example, he will usually try to be diplomatic when confronting people with an unpleasant truth. The risk is that if he is not careful, his desire to soften an expected negative emotional reaction from the hearer by not speaking in a straightforward manner will also diminish the impact of whatever he is sharing. At times, truth needs to be disturbing—especially when sin is being confronted—to bring about the necessary change of heart and direction.

Another major characteristic of the spiritual DNA of a teacher is that the blessings he passes on to others is intergenerational. The added beneficial aspect of his gift is that those he instructs become his spiritual children, who, in turn, teach others who become the teacher's spiritual grandchildren. And so the process continues down the line.

The effectiveness of endowment gift teachers is related to their recognition that their primary calling is to a close relationship with the Lord so that what they impart is not merely cerebral, but has the "seal of approval" of the Holy Spirit. Providing correct doctrine is an essential role for the teacher, but just as important is the need for fresh insight. In all circumstances, God's anointing should permeate whatever the teacher is sharing, whether expounding on time-tested Bible precepts or sharing the latest personal revelation. When teaching is done this way, it will always be vibrant and produce lasting fruit.

We are living in an age in which people are almost constantly being bombarded with half-truths, propaganda, and disinformation on nearly every side. Thus, this endowment gift is needed now more than ever.

One of the clearest biblical examples of an endowment gift teacher is Ezra—a "man of the Book"—who played an exceptional role in restoring the remnant of Israel after its captivity in Babylon.

Ezra was a seeker after the truth even from his early years. Although most of the Jewish captives in Babylon were backslidden, having forgotten Yahweh and His ways, Ezra was very different. He was an ardent student of the Scriptures who painstakingly compiled a complete collection of the sacred writings after their Babylonian conquerors had destroyed all known copies.

Recognized for his integrity and spiritual authority, Ezra was enabled to organize and lead an entourage of Hebrews to return to Jerusalem from Babylon. After his arrival in the capital of the Jewish homeland, Ezra gathered a great assembly of the remnant of God's people and taught them the Law of Moses. On this momentous occasion, thousands were moved to tears and fell on their faces in repentance for having forsaken the ways of the Lord.

Ezra's passion for the truth and heart for God's people shined through during his entire life. The teaching gift within Ezra enabled him to deliver his countrymen from the spiritual pit into which they had fallen. His life proved to be pivotal in the history of Israel. From the day of the great awakening that he spearheaded until the time of Jesus, the Lord used the teaching gift rather than the gift of the prophet to instruct Israel and steer His children back to Him.

A few of the main strengths of the spiritual DNA of a teacher are that they:

1. are driven by a desire to proclaim truth and share it with others
2. feel concerned that the truth is established in every situation
3. validate truth by checking out the facts
4. are able to present truth in a logical and systematic way
5. require thoroughness
6. aren't easily swayed once they "know that they know" something
7. believe that truth has the intrinsic power to change things
8. have a capacity to bring a generational blessing

A few of the weaknesses of this gifting are a tendency to:

1. develop pride in their intellectual ability
2. operate from a perspective of idealism rather than reality
3. get sidetracked easily by new interests

4. tend to feel unworthy in the role of leadership
5. neglect the practical application of truth
6. present a depth of research or level of detail that is unnecessary
7. present truth in an unbalanced way, taking it to an extreme
8. hesitate to confront sin when it is necessary to do so

HOW MUCH OF AN ENDOWMENT GIFT TEACHER ARE YOU?

Please rate yourself as to how much you identify with being an endowment gift teacher.

As you did in the previous chapters, respond to the following statements as they apply to you. Be sure to add up your score from each statement in the box at the bottom.

> ### Remember
>
> 0 means "**not at all** like me"
> 1 means "**slightly** like me"
> 2 means "**somewhat** like me"
> 3 means "**mostly** like me"
> 4 means "**very much** like me"

1. I like to have proof that what someone is saying or reporting is true.

2. I am very aware of factual details and will notice discrepancies in what others say or write.

3. I usually wait until others have had their say and I have had a chance to think it all out before I say or do anything.

4. It really bothers me when someone quotes Scripture out of context or distorts or misinterprets its meaning.

5. I'm not easily persuaded, but once I've explored a matter thoroughly, I will hold onto the viewpoint unless significant new facts or circumstances come to my attention.

6. I like to present facts in a clear, orderly fashion that is backed up by adequate evidence.

7. I usually base my decisions on logical, objective facts not on emotions or opinions.

8. Many times I find it difficult to get in touch with my emotions.

9. Because I am willing to search out the truth I usually won't let something go until I get to the bottom of the matter.

10. Before I take a position on an issue, I like to investigate the facts as thoroughly as possible and evaluate them.

11. I have the ability to examine complex information and issues and explain them to others in an understandable way.

12. I place a high value on the truth because I believe it has an intrinsic power to change people and their circumstances.

TOTAL SCORE: ENDOWMENT GIFT TEACHER

Chapter 10

THE SPIRITUAL DNA OF AN ENCOURAGER (EXHORTER)

"Finally then, brethren, we urge and exhort in the Lord Jesus that you should abound more and more, just as you received from us how you ought to walk and to please God." (1 Thessalonians 4:1, NKJV)

Those with the spiritual DNA of an encourager are particularly equipped to encourage, uplift, and inspire others. Their personality is upbeat, friendly, and outgoing, and they are almost always able to maintain a positive attitude. These attributes attract others to them, and they have an uncommon capacity to reach across barriers and connect with all sorts of people.

By nature, exhorters approach people as if they believe there is no such thing as a stranger. In fact, most encouragers can talk to just about anybody, anywhere, at any time, for any reason. Given their affable nature, it's not surprising that many evangelists, politicians, and salesmen are gifted as exhorters.

Another aspect of an encourager's bundle of God-given abilities is his skill to communicate effectively and influence people both on a personal level and in a group setting. The combination of genuine empathy, ability with words, and an innate capacity to discern people's spiritual needs and level of development cause him not only to relate well with others but to be very persuasive.

If an encourager is inclined to do personal or marriage counseling, these strengths enable him to sway attitudes and sentiments such that he can sometimes achieve a breakthrough that would be extremely difficult for a counselor endowed with any other grace package to obtain.

In the pulpit, an encourager's style of delivery is notably different from that of an endowment gift teacher. The exhorters' primary goal in preaching or teaching is to reach people's hearts. Their favored style, therefore, is more emotional than cerebral. Teachers, on the other hand, will come across with less emotion because their main objective is to engage people's minds as much, if not more, than their hearts. While these two gifts balance each other in their strengths, a person with either of these giftings should recognize that both the heart and the mind need to be addressed whenever they teach or preach—that is, *if* they are to maximize their effectiveness and bring about the kingdom results the Lord desires.

We must also note a negative tendency in encouragers that arises on occasion. Because an exhorter's focus can become results-driven, they may be tempted to use Scripture out of context in order to increase the impact of their message. Anyone who bends the clear meaning of Scripture, however, either in its interpretation or application, has fallen prey to the deception that somehow the "end justifies the means." This mistaken notion is dangerous for the health and welfare of the body of Christ. The integrity of the Word must *always* be respected and upheld, particularly because in these Last Days the spirit of apostasy is now insinuating itself into some churches that in the past were doctrinally solid.

On the positive side of this gifting, one of the healthy exhorter's main interests is to inspire people to develop the God-given potential within them. His primary focus is on people-building and in the practical application of truth. As such, he has little use for theory or abstract ideas. His general approach toward counseling and preaching is not only to confront people with their need for change but also to provide them with an easily understood, concrete means of doing so. This results-oriented approach oftentimes will involve simple action steps that, when implemented, will bring about the desired outcome.

> *One of the main interests of an encourager is to inspire people to develop the God-given potential within them.*

Another feature of exhorters' spiritual makeup is that they typically accept people the way they are because of their empathy as well as their understanding that we are all "works in progress." This non-judgmental attitude is part of the encourager's desire to help people advance in their spiritual development and overcome obstacles so that they can live a full, meaningful life.

The Apostle Barnabas is one of the most outstanding examples of an encourager in the Scriptures. He is first mentioned in the Book of Acts shortly after the day of Pentecost, where we discover that although his birth name was Joseph, the other apostles decided to nickname him "Barnabas," which means "son of encouragement."[1] Given the fierce persecution the church was experiencing in Jerusalem during its early days, Barnabas was no doubt given his nickname not only because of a sunny disposition but also because his positive outlook and words of encouragement were able to cheer and uplift others.

Various episodes in the Book of Acts attest to the fact that Barnabas was used mightily by the Lord throughout his ministry. Being an encourager, he took the fledgling apostle, Saul, later known as the Apostle Paul, under his wing and mentored him at length on several occasions. He also played a key role in the spiritual development of his young cousin, John Mark, whom many scholars identify as the author of the Gospel of Mark. Clearly, Barnabas' encouragement and mentoring had a major impact on both of these men of God as borne out in their own exploits for God's kingdom after having received his counsel and instruction.

Barnabas was the type to stay positive and remain steadfast in the face of opposition and adversity. He spearheaded a fledgling congregation in the pagan city of Antioch, and it wasn't long before the work there was flourishing greatly. Due to his spiritual guidance the church there became one of the most influential churches in the ancient world—second only to the church in Jerusalem.

No doubt Barnabas' spiritual DNA as an exhorter made him an effective preacher and evangelist. Thus, the Scriptures describe him as "full of the Holy Spirit and strong in faith."[2] He was confident and Spirit-filled. With this combination mixed with his grace package it is easy to understand why the church grew rapidly under his tutelage and he was successful in presenting the Gospel to the Gentiles, planting churches in Asia Minor, Cyprus, Syria, and elsewhere.

A few of the main strengths of those with encourager spiritual DNA are that they:

1. are the type of people who "never met a stranger"
2. are attuned to people's feelings
3. are driven to see spiritual growth take place in others
4. are good at inspiring and motivating people
5. see application as the main reason for truth or facts
6. make decisions easily and are spontaneous and flexible
7. are good at bringing reconciliation
8. enjoy and are good at personal counseling

A few of the weaknesses of this gifting are a tendency to:

1. use scriptures out of context to make a point
2. manipulate people's emotions and use deception for selfish gain
3. jump into new projects without finishing existing ones
4. lead by consensus rather than seeking God's guidance and will

5. be inclined to oversimplify problems
6. give up on a counselee who takes more time and effort than expected
7. be so busy encouraging others that family life suffers
8. drift into self-deception and immorality

HOW MUCH OF AN ENCOURAGER ARE YOU?

Please rate yourself as to how much you identify with being an endowment gift encourager.

As you did in the previous chapters, respond to the following statements as they apply to you. Be sure to add up your score from each statement in the box at the bottom.

> ### Remember
>
> 0 means "**not at all** like me"
> 1 means "**slightly** like me"
> 2 means "**somewhat** like me"
> 3 means "**mostly** like me"
> 4 means "**very much** like me"

1. I like being around other people and can relate to them easily.

2. I am normally thought of as an optimist.

3. When problems happen to me or others, I think of how God could use it to help us become stronger Christians.

4. I like to discuss my thoughts with others. Feedback is important.

5. I have a good ability to motivate people to reach their potential and become all that God wants them to be.

☐   6. In counseling and meetings I am able to help people by suggesting steps they can follow to help them grow.

☐   7. I enjoy talking to or counseling with people one on one.

☐   8. I use life examples to illustrate ideas or scriptural concepts all the time.

☐   9. I communicate well. People say I'm a good listener or offer good advice.

☐   10. I have the ability to shoot an arrow of truth into a person's heart while remaining tactful and encouraging.

☐   11. I am rarely judgmental.

☐   12. I like to know what is going on around me and like to be in the middle of everything.

☐   **TOTAL SCORE: ENCOURAGER**

Notes

[1] Acts 4:36. Barnabas is referred to as an apostle in Acts 14:14 and 1 Corinthians 9:5-6.
[2] Acts 11:24, NLT.

Chapter 11

THE SPIRITUAL DNA OF A GIVER (SHARER)

"Share what you have with God's people who are in need. Be hospitable."(Romans 12:13, GW)

A key to understanding the spiritual makeup of a giver is knowing that a person with this grace package has a heart for meeting people's needs combined with special abilities to serve as a "conduit of provision."

Because of their spiritual DNA, most givers share joyfully and generously from whatever is at their disposal—whether it's a bed for a visiting evangelist to sleep on, a bowl of soup for someone who's hungry, or funds to support a worthy project. Their desire is to be an instrument of blessing, and what they share or give depends on the need of the person being helped and the resources available to the giver. But, whatever the situation may be, the givers' heartfelt attitude is that they are "blessed to be a blessing."

The God-given nature of most sharers frequently enables them to see needs that other people may overlook. Once givers identify a need, if they don't personally have the resources required, they will usually take the lead in seeking them out. Part of their grace package includes an extraordinary ability in this area. Because givers are continually operating in a spirit of generosity, which means that they are regularly practicing the biblical principle of "give, and it will be given unto you,"[1] they are operating with the favor of God's blessing on them—which equips them to tap into resources they don't have but are seeking.

Distinguishing between a person with an innate disposition to provide resources to meet others' needs, and who is blessed with prosperity to do so, and another individual who operates according a kingdom principle that leads to increase enables us to more fully appreciate the exceptional qualities of this gift-package. For example, a believer who has learned about the importance of tithing and giving will be blessed by having "more than enough" because they are operating according to a spiritual law. A person with the spiritual DNA of a sharer, however, who is motivated by a spirit of generosity, which is at the very heart of this grace package, is operating on more than merely a biblical principle.

God's favor will be upon both of these people, but givers have exceptional abilities that are part of their spiritual makeup. For example, givers will somehow find a way to hold their own or even prosper in a time of economic downturn while others are falling. In fact, they have an anointing to do so!

As a general rule, a sharer's gift package also includes uncommon stewardship abilities. Most givers have a special knack for making wise purchases and investments. Furthermore, they are endowed with wisdom on how to manage their resources and maximize the impact of their giving. One area in which this is manifested is in the way that givers are usually not gullible when someone tries to manipulate them into giving. Also, once they have contributed to a project, a sharer wants to know that the resources are being used effectively.

A healthy sharer's focus isn't on the accumulation of assets but rather on the distribution of them . They look to the Lord as their source and believe that He will supply their needs. Their purpose is to serve as a conduit through which blessings flow, and should they ever be tempted to block that flow by holding onto that which is meant for others, they have fallen into a carnal trap.

When such a problem arises in a giver, its root is found many times in a lack of trust in the true Giver. Fear and doubt about His provision for their own future can be vanquished only by drawing nearer to the Lord and trusting in His promise to supply their every need.

Also, the spiritual DNA of a giver has the potential for a generational blessing within it. In the biblical account of Abraham, the "father of our faith," we can clearly see this special aspect of the giver's anointing.[2] When Abraham was at the ripe old age of 75,

> *The example of the patriarch Abraham shows that the spiritual DNA of a giver has tremendous potential to bless future generations.*

the Lord instructed him to move with his family to a far off land from Mesopotamia. Yahweh told Abraham that if he did so, He would bless Abraham and enable him to become a blessing to others. This pledge ended with the amazing promise that through him "all the families of the earth would be blessed![3] Indeed, even up until this day, those who are the spiritual sons of Abraham are experiencing the blessings of Abraham as God promised.

Scripture records numerous incidents in Abraham's life in which he demonstrated the characteristics of someone whose spiritual DNA is that of a giver. For example, when a severe famine was afflicting Canaan, Abraham and his family picked up stakes and went to Egypt. That decision proved to be auspicious because Abraham ended up prospering in Egypt during a time when nearly everyone else was suffering from hardship and loss. In fact, God's favor was upon him such that when Abraham returned to Canaan, he and his nephew, Lot, had so much cattle that there wasn't enough grazing land for both of their herds.

Although Abraham was the patriarch of the clan, rather than taking the best land for himself, he asked Lot to pick whatever grazing land he wanted and he, Abraham, would take what was left over. That incredible act of generosity showed that Abraham's confidence was in the Lord, not in riches.

Hospitality is another aspect of the spiritual DNA of a sharer. When Abraham was visited by three strangers in the middle of the day, he eagerly greeted them and gave them the royal treatment. Though he had hundreds of servants, Abraham selected a fatted calf, and his wife, Sarah, prepared the rest of the meal, which they personally served to their guests.

In short, Abraham proved throughout his life to be both generous and hospitable.

A few of the main strengths of those with the spiritual DNA of a giver are that they:

1. have an ability to prosper even in adversity
2. look to God as their source of supply
3. are motivated to provide resources—money, possessions, time, etc.—to help others and advance the kingdom of God
4. handle finances with wisdom and frugality
5. are wise about their giving—not easily manipulated
6. are non-confrontational by nature and will go around barriers
7. hope that their gift is an answer to prayer
8. have a potential to be a generational blessing

A few of the weaknesses of this gifting are a tendency to:

1. look to possessions or money as a source of security, trusting in riches more than in the Lord
2. use financial giving to get out of other responsibilities
3. use possessions to try to control others
4. feel guilty about personal assets
5. lack gratitude for what God has bestowed
6. become insensitive or indifferent to the needs of others
7. be focused more on temporal things than on the kingdom of God
8. become proud in their ability to accumulate finances and assets

HOW MUCH OF A GIVER ARE YOU?

Please rate yourself as to how much you identify with being an endowment gift giver.

As you did in the previous chapters, respond to the following statements as they apply to you. Be sure to add up your score from each statement in the box at the bottom.

> ### Remember
>
> 0 means "**not at all** like me"
> 1 means "**slightly** like me"
> 2 means "**somewhat** like me"
> 3 means "**mostly** like me"
> 4 means "**very much** like me"

1. It brings me a genuine sense of contentment—even joy—when I'm able to give or share what I have with others.

2. I am happy to remain anonymous when I give.

3. I love to see someone receive a gift that they really need or want.

4. I am able to notice when someone has a valid financial need that others have overlooked, and I want to help them.

5. It is a joy to know that my gift is an answer to prayer.

6. When I give a gift to someone I care about, I put a lot of thought into it, and it is important to me that it is of high quality.

7. I think it is very important to give joyfully. I believe God has given me all I have and trust that He will provide for me.

☐ 8. I want the ministries I support to be as effective as possible in spreading the Gospel.

☐ 9. I handle finances with wisdom and frugality, and I have a natural and effective business ability.

☐ 10. I use my giving to set a good example and to motivate others to give.

☐ 11. I am able to see resources where others cannot and put them to use to meet needs.

☐ 12. I am usually discerning when it comes to appeals for money and am not easily fooled or manipulated.

☐ **TOTAL SCORE: GIVER**

Notes

[1] Luke 6:38.
[2] See Acts 7:2, Romans 4:16, and James 2:21.
[3] Genesis 12:1-3.

Chapter 12

THE SPIRITUAL DNA OF A LEADER (ADMINISTRATOR)

"So Jesus called them together and said, 'You know that the rulers in this world lord it over their people, and officials flaunt their authority over those under them. But among you it will be different. Whoever wants to be a leader among you must be your servant...'" (Mark 10:42-43, NLT)

An endowment gift leader is someone with an exceptional ability to shape the future because of an extraordinary array of aptitudes and skills contained in their God-given grace package. These innate abilities enable them to clearly visualize the future, map out the goals and means to get there, motivate people to pitch in by actively taking part, and then coordinate the manpower and mobilize the resources to make the vision become a reality.

The leadership spiritual DNA causes others to regard them as "born leaders." This perception arises at times because leaders have a seeming innate ability to make a difficult job look easy. Moreover, they are the kind of person that, when placed into a group setting in which there is a leadership vacuum, will normally be the one who either takes charge right away or eventually emerges as the *de facto* or formally recognized leader. Furthermore, since the Creator is the One who has given them their gift package, whenever leaders accept their role in fulfilling God's plans, they will experience an extra measure of anointing and favor.

The leader personality is both forceful and tenacious. Considering that anyone who leads a group or organization is at times subject to being the target of strong verbal attacks and determined opposition, leaders must be able to "take the heat," maintain their focus on their priorities, and keep on moving. Spiritually mature leaders must be "thick skinned" in the face of criticism. Only a carnal leader, however, is the sort to "keep score" of wrongs done against them and then to underhandedly plot a retaliation against their detractors.

Loyalty is a significant attribute of the healthy administrator. Such leaders are steadfast to those who work with them and expect loyalty from others in return. As a general rule, they would rather have a trustworthy person working for them than someone else, perhaps more qualified, whom the leader perceives as being less reliable. Moreover, they would rather have fewer people working with them, the ones they can count on, than more, some of whom are likely to be untrustworthy.

Authority and dominion are also a vital aspect of the administrator's spiritual DNA. Leaders are keenly aware of the need to be under authority as well as to exercise their own authority. Because of this, a spiritually mature leader will have little problem "playing second fiddle" to the person over them because they understand and appreciate the importance of honoring authority. Such persons are well aware that their own success as an administrator, in fact, depends to a great extent on others respecting the leader's own authority.

One thing is sure: If the Lord has endowed you with the spiritual DNA of a leader, you have a good understanding of human nature. Because of this key feature, you are more capable of motivating people to work together toward a shared goal and have the needed insight to properly delegate authority and to do that which is necessary to keep the group effort on track and moving forward.

Another aspect of a leader's bundle of God-given abilities is that they think strategically and will not lose sight of the overall picture even when they are in the thick of things. Always keeping their goal in mind, they continually assess the over-all state of affairs and make adjustments to the program or personnel accordingly. Their priority is to see the endeavor come

> *Someone with the spiritual DNA of a leader has exceptional insight into human nature and is capable of motivating people to work together toward a common goal.*

to a successful conclusion as quickly and efficiently as possible.

Endowment gift leaders are also wired to be decision makers. This quality is due to their disposition to avoid procrastination and not get bogged down in the details of a project. Because they constantly maintain a perspective from which they are able to "see the forest through the trees," they can be counted upon to be decisive even when it is difficult.

Another feature of their gift package is that mature leaders have a genuine enthusiasm for whatever they are involved in or have initiated. Their zeal for the project is vital because it greatly influences those who have come on board with them and are working jointly toward a common goal. Due to the administrator's goal-orientation, however, they will already have set their sights as well as invested part of their emotions on their next project long before the current one comes to a conclusion.

Nehemiah was one of the best examples of an endowment gift leader in the Bible.[1] Though he occupied a high position in the Persian Empire and had never been to Jerusalem, from the time he realized that the walls of the Holy City were in ruins he became singled-minded about restoring them and bringing an end to the shame of his people, the Hebrews.

After receiving great favor and generous backing from the king of Persia, Nehemiah journeyed to Jerusalem and immediately surveyed the dismal state of the ruined walls of the city. He did so secretly at night so as to avoid provoking opposition to his efforts. This was a wise approach, and after completing his survey and assessing the required effort to make the needed repairs, he assembled the citizenry of the fallen city and informed them of the vision and plan that had been birthed within him.

Nehemiah proved to be so effective in motivating the people that when he finished addressing them their wholehearted response was, "Yes, let's rebuild the wall!"[2]

Nehemiah demonstrated great skill in organizing the necessary materials as well as keen insight into human nature throughout the whole rebuilding effort. He broke the large-scale building project into small sections and assigned a team to be responsible for each part of the wall.

In the face of the mockery, opposition, and intrigue from a Samaritan leader and his fellow accomplices who were intent on stopping the construction, Nehemiah proved to be imperturbable and steadfastly dedicated to his God-given purpose. He never once wavered in his sense of mission and refused to be delayed or driven off course.

A few of the main strengths of those with the leader or administrator spiritual DNA are that they:

1. are natural and capable leaders
2. are able to envision the finished project
3. need loyalty to and confidence from those under them or over them
4. are task oriented—find their greatest fulfillment and joy in working to accomplish goals
5. are able to be decisive
6. are able to set and maintain priorities
7. enjoy working with and being around people
8. express ideas in ways that communicate clearly

A few of the weaknesses of this gifting are a tendency to:

1. come across as arrogant or overly self-confident
2. view people as "resources" to be used—manipulate others to achieve their personal goals

3. have difficulty working under the authority of someone else
4. make others feel belittled, alienated, incompetent, or inadequate
5. avoid personal responsibilities by delegating them to others
6. develop pride in their own abilities
7. respond to opposition or criticism by seeking to retaliate
8. be inflexible—have difficulty adjusting plans so that the Holy Spirit is allowed to preside

HOW MUCH OF A LEADER OR ADMINISTRATOR ARE YOU?

Please rate yourself as to how much you identify with being an endowment gift leader.

As you did in the previous chapters, respond to the following statements as they apply to you. Be sure to add up your score from each statement in the box at the bottom.

Remember

0 means "**not at all** like me"
1 means "**slightly** like me"
2 means "**somewhat** like me"
3 means "**mostly** like me"
4 means "**very much** like me"

---

1. I have the ability to see the big picture. I can organize resources effectively and recognize people's strengths.

2. I delegate tasks well. I know what can and cannot be delegated.

3. I can break down major objectives into smaller, achievable tasks on which an individual or team can work.

☐   4. I like to encourage and inspire people with cheerfulness, praise, approval, and challenges.

☐   5. If no authority exists, I will step in to pick up the slack. Lack of leadership bothers me.

☐   6. I am not easily swayed by peer pressure, criticism, or complaints.

☐   7. I like working with people and can communicate clearly.

☐   8. I'm good at multi-tasking. I can mentally organize complicated scenarios.

☐   9. I look for people who are hard workers, optimistic, and loyal.

☐   10. I get great joy out of working to see all the parts come together in a finished project.

☐   11. I have the ability to see patterns where others only see complexity.

☐   12. I am a self-starter and decisive.

☐   **TOTAL SCORE: LEADER**

Notes

[1] Book of Nehemiah.
[2] Nehemiah 2:18, NLT.

Chapter 13

THE SPIRITUAL DNA OF A MERCY GIVER

"But the wisdom from above is pure first of all; it is also peaceful, gentle, and friendly; it is full of compassion and produces a harvest of good deeds; it is free from prejudice and hypocrisy." (James 3:17, GNB)

A person with the mercy giver spiritual DNA is compassionate and has an uncommon degree of empathy for people when they are hurting or downtrodden.

Compared with any of the other gift bundles, a compassion-graced person normally has the least amount of difficulty finding the heart of God in any given situation. In fact, their spiritual makeup causes them to be much more at ease being led by their hearts rather than their heads.

If you are a mercy giver you will find yourself being drawn to the kinds of people whom many others will try to avoid or even run away from—the underdog, the outcast, and those in distress. Because of your compassionate nature you have probably discovered that those who are hurting or lonely tend to be drawn to you as well. Your kind and gentle disposition has attracted them just as if you are a magnet. Just a caution, however: There are some who may see your caring personality as a weakness they can take advantage of, even to the point of trying to deceive you.

People with mercy giver spiritual DNA tend to be more spontaneous than others. Many are able to express their emotions freely, and some have a flair for creativity as well. Though it isn't always the case, many intuitive, "artistic types" are endowed with this grace package.

Typical mercy-givers have personalities that are cheerful and outgoing and, as might be expected, are usually well-liked and have many friends. Most of the time they are good listeners and are careful to avoid saying anything that might hurt someone's feelings. As such, they come across as unassuming and peaceable. Although they may usually appear to be light-hearted, compassion-graced people have a thoughtful, serious side as well.

One of the major characteristics of the mercy giver grace package is that they are nearly always non-judgmental. This quality can be both a strength and a weakness, however. On the positive side, they are the first to offer a shoulder to cry on, a listening ear to the lonely, and comfort to the hurting. But in some instances the soul who is being helped needs a dose of the truth as well. Oftentimes, the reason for people's pain or the cause of their affliction is their sinful state, and a mercy giver is the least likely person to deliver such a message.

Someone with the spiritual DNA of a mercy giver will be the first to offer a shoulder to cry on, a listening ear to the lonely, and comfort to the hurting.

A mercy giver has an innate God-given quality to discern and relate to feelings that are at work in other people's minds and hearts. Often upon walking into a room he can sense the spiritual or emotional tone of an individual or a group, which is a trait he has in common with the endowment gift prophet. This particular sensitivity typically means that a spiritually mature mercy giver has an easier time than others being "in tune" with the heart of God.

While empathy is a major asset of this gifting, it can become problematic for some compassion-graced people if they over-identify with the person who is hurting. In some cases, mercy givers may become downcast or despondent over the situation of the person with whom they are commiserating. In fact, they can even end up suffering almost as much as the person whom they are supposedly helping.

Ironically, though mercy givers are generally very tolerant and charitable, if a person says something they deem harsh or critical about the individual they are helping, mercy givers may lash out at the critic for his lack of sympathy. They may even end up harboring a long-lasting grudge.

Though the Gospels do not provide us with much detail about the life of Mary, the mother of Jesus Christ, it is apparent that her primary gifting was that of a mercy giver.

First of all, consider that Mary was chosen to carry a child who would be thought of by those in the local community, Nazareth, as born out of wedlock. A mercy giver—especially one whose heart is in tune with God's heart—would have the least difficulty carrying out such an assignment. To be sure, there were neighbors who judged Mary and Joseph for their supposed sin and perhaps murmured about them. But, as Jesus said in the Sermon on the Mount, "Blessed are the merciful, because they will be shown mercy."[1] Revealingly, there is no scriptural evidence that Jesus' family was socially ostracized during His early years.

We also catch a glimpse of Mary's spontaneity and creativity, which also are traits of a mercy giver. It was these qualities and her spiritual sensitivity that moved her to lift her voice in a spiritual song while visiting with her cousin Elizabeth after finding out she was pregnant.[2] Mary's words flowed as the Holy Spirit moved upon her, testifying of the mercy and greatness of the Lord.

In light of Mary's compassionate nature, we can better understand the dynamic that occurred between her and Jesus at the wedding feast in Cana. When she asked Him to do something about the predicament of the wedding host's having run out of wine, she did so because she identified with the dilemma of the groom's family and wanted to spare them from being humiliated. Though it is clear from Jesus' response that He considered Mary's request to be ill-timed, He knew her spur-of-the-moment plea was out of the goodness of her heart and, therefore, obliged.

A few of the main strengths of those with the mercy giver spiritual DNA are that they:

1. are attracted to people who are hurting or in distress and "feel" for them
2. have a desire to remove hurts and bring comfort and healing
3. are ruled by their hearts and not their heads
4. sense the spiritual or emotional atmosphere of a group or in an individual
5. have a supernatural ability to love and care for others, even strangers
6. are careful with words and actions to avoid hurting others
7. are intuitive and "soft"— are into hugs
8. are magnets for people who are going through mental and emotional distress

A few of the weaknesses of this gifting are a tendency to:

1. fail to establish and maintain prudent boundaries with others
2. be indecisive
3. be so accommodating and non-judgmental that they become enablers of sinful behavior
4. be overly idealistic and subjective, which can lead to poor judgment
5. become depressed or inwardly grieve because of their empathy with others' problems
6. be overly sensitive and easily wounded in exercising their gift
7. be emotionally vulnerable and easily taken advantage of or manipulated
8. be a magnet for disturbed individuals and rebellious types who have issues with authority

HOW MUCH OF A MERCY GIVER ARE YOU?

Please rate yourself as to how much you identify with being an endowment gift mercy giver.

As you did in the previous chapters, respond to the following statements as they apply to you. Be sure to add up your score from each statement in the box at the bottom.

> ### Remember
>
> 0 means "**not at all** like me"
> 1 means "**slightly** like me"
> 2 means "**somewhat** like me"
> 3 means "**mostly** like me"
> 4 means "**very much** like me"

1. I am drawn to those suffering emotionally, and they are often drawn to me.

2. I want to do whatever I can to remove the hurt from people's lives.

3. I am sensitive to words, attitudes, or actions that may hurt others.

4. I can often sense intuitively if someone is covering up sorrow, pain, anger, or other emotions.

5. I am a very intuitive person and I'll admit it— sometimes I'm not very objective.

6. I get very upset when someone I care about has been hurt. I want to help alleviate their burdens.

7. I am tolerant and not judgmental. I welcome friendships

with all sorts of people.

[ ] 8. I prefer to have deep friendships with mutual commitment over superficial ones.

[ ] 9. I like to pray for and with those who are hurting. I feel like God is working through me when someone needs me.

[ ] 10. I am usually thought of as an optimist and always try to look for the good in people.

[ ] 11. I am drawn to people who are in distress, and I have an unusual ability to comfort them.

[ ] 12. I avoid being firm or confrontational and usually have difficulty speaking the truth to people so as to not hurt their feelings.

[ ] **TOTAL SCORE: MERCY GIVER**

Notes

[1]Matthew 5:7, HCSB.
[2]See Luke 1:46-55.

Chapter 14

EVALUATING YOUR ENDOWMENT GIFTING

HOW DID YOU DO?

A t this point, you should have all of your total scores from your responses at the end of each of the chapters that describe the seven endowment gifts in detail (chapters 7-13). If you haven't finished that process, please do it now.

Once you've obtained a total score for each one of the endowment gifts you likely have a good idea of which of them are your two or three strongest ones. If that is the case, great!

In this chapter, we're going to "fine tune" those scores by determining your likely reaction to two different hypothetical situations. Before looking at those please fill in the blanks below with the total score you already obtained for each of the seven endowment gifts:

Chapter 7   Prophet: _____

Chapter 8   Server: _____

Chapter 9   Teacher: _____

Chapter 10   Encourager: _____

Chapter 11   Giver: _____

Chapter 12   Leader: _____

Chapter 13   Mercy-Giver: _____

If your top two scores are very close (within a few points), or if your third or fourth highest scores are only slightly lower, your likely responses to the "spilled coffee scenario" and the "community outreach scenario" below should help you determine your two strongest gifts from the others.

SCENARIO INSTRUCTIONS

In the two fictional circumstances below, choose what your **most likely** response would be and what your **second most likely** response would be.

Read the first scenario—about reacting to a spilled cup of coffee—and then decide which of the seven possible responses is your *most likely* one and which is your *second most likely* response. After deciding, give 2 points to your most likely response by writing the number "2" in the box next it and then write a "1" in the box next to your second most likely response. Then score all the other response boxes with a "0." If by chance you don't know what your second most likely response would be, then score only your most likely one with a "2" and score all the others "0."

Once you have done this for the spilled coffee scenario do the same for the community outreach scenario.

Remember!

2 = your most likely response
1 = for a second most likely response (if you have one)
0 = for all the other responses

A.) Spilled Coffee Scenario: *You are sitting at a table eating a meal with a group of friends. One of them knocks over a full mug of coffee, and it spills all over the table and floor. Would you say?*

☐ 1. "That's what happens when you're not careful!"

☐ 2. "Oh! Let me help you clean this mess up."

☐ 3. "The reason your coffee spilled was because you set it too close to the edge."

☐ 4. "Next time, let's set your coffee closer to the center where it won't get knocked over. OK?"

☐ 5. "Don't worry. I'll be happy to share some of my coffee with you."

☐ 6. "I'll get a rag. Jesse, you go get a mop. Becky, help pour a new cup of coffee."

☐ 7. "Don't feel bad. It could happen to anyone."

B.) Community Outreach Scenario: *Your church has widely publicized a community outreach event that will be held at a nearby park and the*

deadline for getting everything ready is fast approaching. More volunteers
are needed to make sure that everything is organized and the preparations
are completed on time. When just a few volunteers show up, what would
you most likely do or say? ....

☐ 1. Announce to the group that "***Everyone*** from the church should be here helping out, and there really are ***no*** excuses."

☐ 2. Roll up your sleeves and work until late at night to make sure everything gets done.

☐ 3. Try to convince everyone of the importance of what they are doing by reminding them they are part of fulfilling the Great Commission.

☐ 4. Exclaim: "Hey everybody! Come on! The job is almost done. We can do it!"

☐ 5. Go out and buy doughnuts and coffee for the group to make sure everybody stays until the job is done.

☐ 6. Start calling other church members to get more help and then organize them when they show up.

☐ 7. Remind everyone how much the people in the community are hurting and really need God.

ADDING IT ALL UP

You're almost done now. What remains is adding your scores from each of the two hypothetical scenarios to the scores you had already obtained from your responses at the end of chapters 7 through 13.

YOUR ENDOWMENT GIFT SCORES

Chapter Total Scores	Spilled Coffee Response Scores	Community Out-reach Response Scores	Combined Scores (Columns 1-3)
Ch. 7 (Prophet) _____	1. _____	1. _____	1. Prophet _____
Ch. 8 (Server) _____	2. _____	2. _____	2. Server _____
Ch. 9 (Teacher) _____	3. _____	3. _____	3. Teacher _____
Ch. 10 (Encourager) _____	4. _____	4. _____	4. Encourager _____
Ch. 11 (Giver) _____	5. _____	5. _____	5. Giver _____
Ch. 12 (Leader) _____	6. _____	6. _____	6. Leader _____
Ch. 13 (Mercy-Giver) _____	7. _____	7. _____	7. Mercy-Giver _____

Simply mark your scores from each exercise as indicated in the first three columns. Once you've done that, add the three scores in each row and mark your total in the fourth column. That gives you an overall, combined score from the three exercises.

INTERPRETING YOUR RESULTS

In the "Combined Scores" above, the gift for which you scored the highest is your primary or predominant gift. Most who take the test will find that one score is significantly higher than the rest. When that is the case, it is clear what your strongest gifting is.

Many also find that there is a second gift for which they score significantly higher than any of the five remaining gifts. When that is the case, that second highest score represents their secondary gifting.[1]

While most people have one or two endowment gift scores that emerge as significantly higher than the rest, that situation is not always the case. For some, a pattern will emerge in which their strengths are more evenly distributed among several gifts. If that proves to be the case for you, your primary gifting is still your highest score—it's just not as dominant in your overall gift array.

When considering the particular combination of grace packages that comprise your unique spiritual DNA, your main focus should be on your strengths—that is, your top one

> *In evaluating the spiritual DNA that is uniquely yours, your main focus should be on your strengths—that is, your top one or two endowment gifts.*

or two endowment gifts. The reason for this is that the Lord gave you those particular graces in an extra measure so that you could fulfill the destiny He has for you as well as fit into a special niche He has for you in ministering within the body of Christ.

Notes

[1]Also, in certain exceptional cases, there may be a third endowment gift that scores much higher than the other four. When that happens, this is the person's tertiary gift.

Chapter 15

YOUR STRENGTHS IN ACTION

"Just as our bodies have many parts and each part has a special function, so it is with Christ's body. We are many parts of one body, and we all belong to each other." (Romans 12: 4, 5, NLT)

Identifying your two strongest endowment gifts that provide the basic pattern and dominant elements of your spiritual DNA is a significant accomplishment. As you take the time to reflect on the fundamental strengths and innate abilities God has placed within you, you will gain fresh insight about your true identity and God-ordained purpose in life.

Properly appreciated, such new understanding will help you discern your personal mission and the types of undertakings for which you are most suited. The Holy Spirit, who leads and guides God's children in all truth, will help you sort things out and find a clearer direction. He will not only reveal to you where you should be headed in life but also help you find your proper place in the body of Christ.

Your increased understanding and awareness of who you really are and what you've been made to do will set you toward the destiny that the Lord purposed for you from time immemorial. Now *that* is truly exciting!

JESUS, OUR BEST EXAMPLE

In truth, your personal combination of spiritual DNA is a wonderful reflection of the nature and abilities of your Maker. Since you also inherited a fallen, Adamic nature, however, you are born with limitations on the extent to which your God-given spiritual nature can shine through.

After Adam's fall in the Garden of Eden, only one person has operated without hindrance in the fullness of his spiritual DNA—Jesus Christ, the only-begotten Son of our heavenly Father. He embodied perfection in many ways—not the least of which was by operating in each of the seven endowment gifts to their fullest measure. He showed us what grace can do when it isn't limited by the frailty of fallen human nature.

- As a Prophet, He discerned the hearts of men and understood their motives even better than they did.
- As a Servant, He was unfailing in his loyalty to his Father's purpose and, as the Scripture says, He, "... *did not come to be served, but to serve, and to give his life as a ransom for many.*"[1]
- As a Teacher, He had an incomparable ability to elaborate on the great truths and secrets of God in a way that captured the hearts and minds of both the common folk and the learned.
- As an Encourager, He continually broke down the barriers of carnal thinking that held people captive and challenged all who heard Him to reach for a higher level of spiritual maturity.
- As a Giver, He poured out his life for all, giving us His everything until He drew His very last breath on earth.

- As a Leader, He took dominion and authority over everything that opposed kingdom purposes.
- As a Mercy Giver, He ministered with a heart of compassion to those who were hurting and personified love itself!

In short, Jesus did it all! He is the portrait of perfection.[2]

And no matter what our own endowment gift array looks like, He is our shining example—the One to whom we can look to see how it is to be done—what we should say and do in every situation. Since the ultimate expression of every spiritual gift is personified in Jesus Christ, the more we become like Him, the more we will grow in our own gifting.

WHERE'S YOUR BEST FIT

As we mentioned earlier, the ultimate purpose of your endowment gifting is not merely to fulfill your personal destiny in this world but, in so doing, to glorify your Maker.

During this Age of Grace in which we are living, one of the most significant ways in which a believer can bring glory to the Lord is through active involvement in the body of Christ.

The question most have is: "Where do I fit in?" To be sure, God has a special assignment that is meant just for you! Certainly, it isn't His intention for you or any of His children to be a mere "spectator"—watching others do the "work of the ministry" while sitting idly by on the sidelines.

Your gifting is meant to complement the grace packages of other members in a local church setting so that the body of Christ can reach its full potential together. Your congregation is supposed to work something like a supernatural seven-cylinder engine. For the power of God to be delivered as it should, all seven cylinders must be well-oiled with the anointing of the Lord and

The local church is supposed to work something like a supernatural "seven cylinder" engine—one cylinder for each endowment gift package.

function together according to divine orchestration and direction. If any of the cylinders is misfiring or not working properly, it will be that much more difficult for the body to accomplish His purposes.

THE PROPHET

If you are a prophet, your role is to function as the "eyes" of the church—seeing into the invisible realm of spiritual reality. You are to serve as a "watchman on the wall" who discerns spiritual danger and is unafraid to warn others of the risks of letting sin and unhealthy influences go unchecked.

If you are a prophet, one of the most appropriate places for you in a local congregation may be in the area of intercessory prayer. In fact, to be most effective, every prayer ministry should include at least one mature, prophetically-gifted person, who operates easily in the manifestation gifts of the discerning of spirits, word of knowledge, and word of wisdom.

If you are an endowment-gift prophet who is accustomed to operating in the God-kind of love then you may also be apt to serve in a healing ministry, since the sources of many sicknesses must be spiritually discerned.

Also, if your prophetic "rough edges" have been sufficiently "worn off," and you are musically inclined, then another option is serving with the worship team.

If the leadership of your local congregation recognizes your spiritual DNA as a prophet, then, with the Lord's calling and sufficient maturity, you may be able to serve as an equipping gift prophet — that is, if your local church acknowledges such a ministry.

Even if it does not, however, if you are sufficiently developed as an endowment gift prophet your abilities are critical for the spiritual direction of your church. Whether you are chosen to serve on the governing board or not, you should seek to work with others to steer the church in the right direction as the Lord is leading. With you and your gifting serving in a local body, the church and its members should be able to avoid many traps, dangers, and deceptions that the enemy most assuredly is plotting.

Some of the areas in which the prophetic gift is most needed are:

• intercessory prayer • healing ministry • Bible study leader • serving in leadership • worship team • working with "special needs" groups such as ministering to addicts and in prison ministry • personal and street evangelism

THE SERVER

If you are gifted as a server, you are best suited to function as the "hands" of the body by ministering to practical needs and serving in a support role.

Your gifting ensures that the mundane but essential aspects of ministry are not neglected. There is hardly an activity or program that goes on within your church in which your services as a minister are not vitally needed.

If you are a server, you are the one who is most capable of seeing what needs doing and then helping to get the job done. If you are technically inclined, you may consider working with the teams that run the sound system or in video production. Serving as a greeter or usher is also a good option. You may also be suited to assisting in a small group setting.

If you are ministry-gifted you are one of the most likely to volunteer when food needs to be prepared, chairs need to be set up, someone needs to be visited in the hospital or at home, or when transportation or a driver is needed.

Also, if you are a minister, you are likely to be the type to pitch in and take up responsibilities even if you are doing so in an area of service that isn't quite suitable. Your willingness is simply because something needs doing, and you want to see that whatever it is gets done. In other words, you are willing to "fill in" as required.

Some servers are called especially to help those in leadership. If that is your case, you are able to take care of the necessary details that ensure the smooth functioning of any ministry.

Though you may feel quite uncomfortable in the lead role, as a server you are able to help organize activities, programs, and outreaches. As long as a long-term commitment isn't required, you are suited to see the project through to completion.

There are many areas in which a server is needed in a church. Just a few of those are:

- *nursery attendant* • *church secretary* • *greeting and ushering*
- *teacher's aide* • *cleaning* • *building and grounds maintenance*
- *setting up for services* • *organizing special activities and events*
  • *intercessory prayer* • *administrative assistant*

THE TEACHER

Those with the teaching endowment gift serve as the "mind" of the body of Christ. The focus of this gifting in a church setting is on the teacher's discovering truths from the Word and sharing those spiritual realities with others.

Obviously, teaching is a vital function for the spiritual health of a local assembly. Those who are equipping gift teachers are responsible for doing their part in instructing the saints to do *"the work of the ministry."*[3] Furthermore, babes in the faith as well as youth and those who are mature in the faith need to be taught.

Sunday School is a good place for someone with the teacher spiritual DNA to begin developing their gifting. If you are endowed with this grace package, but have very little teaching experience, one of the best places to start is as a teacher's assistant. The age group with which you become involved in the beginning is not as important as making sure you gear your lessons to the interests of the group. Your responsibility is not only to be accurate in what you teach but also to make the lesson understandable and interesting!

In fact, one of the basic precepts of good teachers is that they maintain in the forefront of their thinking that "unless those being taught have understood the lesson, then teaching really hasn't occurred."[4]

In other words, results count! Merely "throwing out" a slew of information to those you are teaching, hoping that at least some of it will be "caught," is a very poor approach for such an important function in the church as a teaching ministry.

There are usually many opportunities to teach within a local church. But, of course, they depend to an extent on the size, demographics, particular characteristics of your local assembly, and your own interests and abilities. Beyond the obvious needs of Sunday School, you might consider:

> • *teaching (or assisting) in a cell group* • *training young adults*
> • *serving as Bible study leader* • *teaching in a prison ministry*
> • *discipling new believers* • *teaching in a men's or women's group*

THE ENCOURAGER

Those with the encourager spiritual DNA serve as the "mouth" of the body of Christ. Their keen insight into human nature combined with their speaking abilities and desire to see others grow spiritually causes them to inspire others onward.

If you are an exhorter then you likely have not only a "way with words" but the ability to get along with just about anybody. Because of your sunny disposition, you are able to put the church's best foot forward by making a favorable impression on church visitors as a greeter or usher.

Many with the encourager spiritual DNA gravitate toward personal counseling. If that is the case with you, there are many within the body of Christ you can help—either on an informal basis or through an established counseling ministry within your local church. Such counseling can also occur in the setting of a home fellowship.

If you are an encourager, you are motivated by a desire to bolster the morale of God's people and increase their faith level. If church leadership has recognized your gifting, it is likely that at some point you will have opportunities to speak from the pulpit. Whether it's a brief "pep talk" to rouse the faithful to overcome a difficult situation or a more lengthy message to exhort the brothers and sisters to believe for the Lord's favor, you are well able to motivate them to raise their sights.

Evangelism is an area in which an encourager is well suited for service. You have remarkable abilities to persuade others, which, when combined with your facility at presenting the Gospel in a clear and simple way, makes you extremely effective. In other words, the Lord has given you prodigious abilities that enable you to be a great soul winner.

If you have the encourager spiritual DNA, a few of the areas in which you may be suited to serve are:

> • *evangelism* • *counseling* • *leading worship* • *preaching* • *prison ministry* • *greeting or ushering* • *youth ministry* • *discipleship* • *leading a Bible study* • *hospital visitation*

THE GIVER

Givers function as the "arms" of the body of Christ. The spiritual DNA of a person with this grace package enables the church to reach out and accomplish the vision the Lord has revealed to the leadership of the local church.

If you are a giver then your generous nature will inspire others to give as well. Added to that, you can be an invaluable asset in raising funds by speaking up for a project that you support and by encouraging others to contribute to it as well.

Hospitality is part of the grace package for many with this gifting. If this is the case with you, then opening up your home to others brings you great satisfaction—whether it's to facilitate a home fellowship or to give a visitor a place to sleep.

A giver is a "sharer" as well. They are willing to share whatever blessings the Lord has given them with others. Perhaps a young couple in your church needs a car to use for a few months. If you are a giver you will be happy to oblige them if you have an extra car or one that is less needed. When you are cooking, you are the type to make more than enough with the idea that you will be able to feed any other hungry mouths that unexpectedly show up.

Your role in the church is not only in the area of providing resources but also in managing them. Since you know how to be prudent in handling limited resources, you can help your church by serving on a stewardship committee or financial board. Your financial acumen is especially needed if your church is embarking on a building program or contemplating the purchase of real estate.

If you have the giver spiritual DNA a few of the ways you can help your local church are by:

> • *hosting a home fellowship* • *fundraising for special projects* • *serving on a stewardship committee* • *serving as church treasurer* • *contributing to different projects* • *being an advocate for missions* • *opening your home to ministry activities* • *volunteering to help the needy*

THE LEADER

Those with the leader/administrator spiritual DNA serve as the "shoulders" of the body of Christ. Much of the responsibility for moving the people of God forward in the direction in which the Lord is leading falls upon their shoulders.

If this is your grace package, whenever you sense a vacuum of leadership within an area of ministry your natural tendency is to want to fill the gap and assume the responsibility. This inclination is a positive attribute because your gifting brings a sense of direction and order when either is lacking.

With whatever ministry you are involved your leader spiritual DNA enables you to motivate those you are working with to pull together toward a common ministry goal. If you have been chosen or appointed as the head of a ministry, the administrative aspect of your endowment gift gives you the insight necessary to assign tasks and delegate responsibilities to the appropriate brother or sister as well as bring organization to any group that is in disarray.

Being purpose-driven, once you have determined the Lord's direction for the ministry you are leading, your grace package causes you to be committed to following through and taking whatever measures are needed to complete the task or project.

Because you are a strategic thinker who can see the "big picture," you have the potential to bring about needed change and be an effective instrument for advancing the kingdom of God.

Representative examples of areas in which a leader/administrator can serve best in the local congregation are to:

> • *organize church outreaches and projects* • *coordinate church planting* • *lead in any area of ministry to which you've been called* • *serve as Sunday school superintendent, administrative pastor, head deacon, committee chairperson, or church office manager* • *manage church building projects*

THE MERCY GIVER

Those with the mercy giver spiritual DNA serve as the "heart" of the body of Christ—bringing warmth and compassion to the lost and hurting.

Reflecting God's mercy, those graced with this gift package are able to feel right at home in a wide array of ministries in which most churches are involved. They bring warmth to any local congregation because of their caring nature. Any ministry to those who are suffering or in distress is a potential avenue for the operation of this gift. Whether it's working with single mothers, those dealing with addiction, or those suffering from a tragic personal loss, the mercy giver can provide the needed empathy, counsel, and comfort.

If you are a mercy giver, you have a heart for the lost and may want to be involved in outreach beyond the local congregation. This desire can be expressed in a community outreach or even in foreign missions. The simple truth is that suffering humanity is found in every corner of our world, and its needs are met primarily by those with your gifting.

In many cases you will relate to people who are hurting with whom you appear to have very little in common. God moves on your heart to reach out to them in their need, and, as a result, you show them God's mercy and love.

If you are a person with the gift of compassion, you are the one most likely to take the Gospel message and apply it practically by ministering to needy people. You make the Gospel relevant and put your faith into action by touching lives.

Some of the areas of ministry in a local church most suited for a mercy giver are:

• hospital visitation • children's ministry • missions • prison
• addiction recovery • evangelism • victims of abuse • nursery
• counseling • healing • single parents • worship • crisis pregnancy
• reaching generation X or Y • homeless • clothes closet/food
pantry/soup kitchen

WORKING TOGETHER

"How wonderful and pleasant it is when brothers live together in harmony!" (Psalm 133:1, NLT)

It is clear that each one of the gift packages is necessary for a local congregation to fulfill its destiny. Without the mercy givers a church will seem cold and perhaps even "heartless." Without the gift of prophecy to balance the mercy gift it is likely that a church will sink into an attitude of tolerating sin in the body. Without the gift of leadership, a church will lack a clear vision for the future as well as a sense of dynamism.

Without the servers, it will be extremely difficult for the church to even operate. Without the givers, the church won't have the necessary finances or resources to operate. Without the encouragers, the church will be in danger of spiritual stagnation and sterility. Without the gift of the teachers, the church is in danger of drifting from her spiritual moorings and abandoning sound biblical doctrine.

The spiritual DNA of every grace package is essential to the functioning of the local church. When all of the gifts are combined, a corporate anointing is manifested. The church becomes supernaturally energized!

Harmony is vital so that each aspect of the perfect nature of God can operate unhindered. Unity within the body of Christ is enhanced when the role of each endowment gifting is recognized and given its proper place.

When you find your place and operate in the body of Christ as God ordained, you are not only responding to God's will for your life but you also ensuring that His supernatural Bride fulfills her destiny.

> *Every grace package is as essential as it is supernatural. When all of them are combined, a corporate anointing is manifested. The church becomes supernaturally energized!*

Notes

[1] Mark 10:45.

[2] There are at least seven examples in the Gospels of Jesus' operating in each one of the seven endowment gifts. To do such a thing is humanly impossible. In fact, the human mind has difficulty even fathoming such perfection. This is absolute proof that He was indeed God in human form.

[3] Ephesians 4:12.

[4] This principle is an ancient Hebrew one.

Chapter 16

GROWING IN GRACE

SPIRIT LED OR SELF-SUFFICIENT?

"... the love of God has been poured out in our hearts by the Holy Spirit who was given to us." (Romans 5:5, NKJV)

The main focus of our investigation up to this point has been on determining the prominent features of your spiritual DNA and then examining the role the Lord has for you in serving in the body of Christ.

The secret to the church's operating in harmony is this: The God-kind of love abides in the people of God and serves as a great conductor that orchestrates everyone together just as a maestro ensures that the instrumentalists in an orchestra work together to make beautiful music. The degree to which love governs the members of the church determines the extent to which the diversity of gifts can operate in harmony. On the other hand, if members are ruled by the flesh, then the evil works of the flesh will prevail—works such as strife, envy, quarreling, selfish ambition, and division.[1] In other words, just about everything that kills unity and harmony!

On an individual level, your own spiritual growth is determined to a large extent by the degree to which you allow the God-kind of love to rule in your heart. Scripture tells us that the Holy Spirit has poured God's love into our hearts. This type of "pouring" is not a sprinkle or a trickle but rather a Holy Spirit gusher.[2]

If we want to see dynamic spiritual growth then we need to be saturated—fully soaked—in God's presence and filled with His Word. It is vital that the life-producing medium of His love flood our inner man to supernaturally energize our spiritual DNA.

Abiding in our heavenly Father's presence and putting His Word first will produce life-changing results. It will eliminate the carnal or negative aspects of our God-given abilities and cause the positive, spiritual side of our gifting to grow. It is as if the God-kind of love works as a potent fertilizer and weed killer at the same time. Nurtured by this powerful type of love, the positive qualities that were once latent in our spiritual DNA are invigorated, and we grow to become more like Jesus Christ.

ENABLED IN EVERY SITUATION

"Now may the God of peace… equip you with all you need for doing His will. May He produce in you, through the power of Jesus Christ, every good thing that is pleasing to Him." (Hebrews 13:20-21, NLT)

In discerning your calling and place in the body of Christ, it is wise to focus on your strengths—the one or two areas of your spiritual DNA that stand out from the rest. You may be wondering, however, how the remaining grace packages of your gifting fit the overall picture.

While your endowment gift profile is not set in stone, and there is a degree of variability, your weakest gift will never become your strongest one. As you grow closer to the Lord, however, there may be a slight change in the relative strength of one grace package compared with the others, but usually it will be only to meet a particular need. When that happens, the Lord is giving you an added measure of grace to rise to a ministry occasion.

God's children should be led by the Holy Spirit at all times. He has equipped you so that, when needed, you can operate in any of the seven endowment gifts because He has placed His divine nature within you. For example:

- Although your primary grace package may not be that of a **prophet,** you should be ready to proclaim the truth of God's Word to others whenever the opportunity arises.
- Even if your major strength is not that of a **server,** you should always be willing to be of service to others, just as Jesus was.
- While you may not have the endowment gift of a **teacher,** you should be ready at all times to instruct those who are seeking truth.
- Although your primary gifting may not be that of an **encourager,** you should be keenly interested in the spiritual development of your fellow man.
- Even if the strongest aspect of your spiritual DNA is not that of a **giver,** as a child of the Most High you should be inclined to share from that which you possess as the Spirit leads.
- Though your gifting may not be that of a **leader,** you should always be willing to take a stand when others will not.
- Finally, while your primary gifting may not be that of a **mercy giver,** you should be willing to identify with the hurts of others and be ready to care for their needs.

Truly Spirit-led believers look to Jesus as their example in every situation. Because all seven of the endowment gift packages reside within you, you have the potential, to a greater or less extent, to meet any circumstance that comes your way. For example, if you have a special needs child or an elderly parent to care for, as you follow the leading of the Holy Spirit, the gift of compassion will grow within you and become stronger. This is true even if compassion had previously been one of your weaker gift packages. This happens when God's grace causes the latent potential of the mercy giver within you to be energized and grow to meet the need at hand.

Though the basic template of your spiritual DNA was designed before you were born, you can and will grow according to the grace that supplies for every need.

Some believers may seek to excuse carnal behavior because they believe they are limited to operating only in their strongest gifting. As we have seen, however, such notions should never confine or constrain a Spirit-led believer.

Another problem can arise when a child of God is out of balance in his gifting. For all of us, the fulcrum of our grace package is the God-kind of love. It will keep us from the works of the flesh, excess, and extremes. For example, a prophet who tries to justify a judgmental attitude or lack of sensitivity to other people's feelings may be under the misconception that being pleasant or "nice" isn't part of his gift package. Such a person views his role as an "exposer" and a "denouncer"—not as a "restorer." When such a person is operating from a motive of love, however, he will not be negative or rude but rather view his primary purpose as serving as a prophet who reconciles.

RELATING TO OTHERS

"I… urge you to walk worthy of the calling you have received, with all humility and gentleness…." (Ephesians 4:1-2, HCSB)

A natural tendency in most people, including some in the body of Christ, is to assume (1) that many others share their point of view and (2) that those who do not are somehow at fault or flawed (e.g., perhaps they haven't really understood the situation or are not sensitive enough to it).

It is clear, however, that many differences in how people view and react to what is happening around them result from their particular spiritual DNA. Although a variety of factors influence people's differences of opinion and emphasis, one of the most important ones is the personality they were born with, which is determined by the spiritual template used by their Maker.[3]

Diversity is good, and as we observe the profusion of variety found throughout God's creation we understand that it is very much His idea.[4] We were not created to be an "island unto ourselves" but to be part of something much bigger. Because of this, our unique gifting was never meant to be the be-all and end-all of grace packages. It was meant to complement the gifting of others. Each of us is part of a grand mosaic and makes our own irreplaceable contribution to the total pattern.

We need to relate to others on the basis of recognizing and appreciating the God-given gifts within them and by walking in humility, not thinking of ourselves more highly than we should.[5] When we come across

> *When someone's spiritual DNA is different—and even very different—from our own, it should be a cause for celebration because it means that we can now complement each other.*

someone whose spiritual DNA is quite different from our own, we should take it as a cause for celebration because we can now complement each other. Their particular strengths can compensate for some of our weakness and vice versa.

As mentioned above, aside from Jesus Christ, no one has a gift array that is strong in all seven of the endowment giftings. Therefore, in any situation, some people will have a grace package that makes them well-suited to handle it whereas others will have a grace package that makes them not so well suited to handle it.

Take, for example, a scenario in a church in which a certain clique has been spreading gossip despite the pastor's attempts to correct this sin from the pulpit. The gossipers need to be confronted with the truth in a way that brings repentance—that is, godly sorrow and changed behavior.

In such a case, it is obvious that this is not the time to dispatch a mercy giver to handle the situation. The most appropriate type of person to address it is a mature endowment gift prophet—one whose motivation is to bring about restoration.

Let's now consider a few examples of the innumerable ways in which one spiritual DNA is able to complement another. Teachers are an excellent complement for encouragers/exhorters in that they will tend to steer exhorters away from the dangers of deception and error. At the same time, the sunny disposition of the encourager will have a positive impact on a teacher, who may tend to become isolated from others and develop an overly idealistic view of life and the world. A server's gift is usually able to combine in a complementary way with any other gifting. Likewise, the giver's generosity complements the spiritual DNA of all the other gifts in a positive way. The tendency of some givers to be aloof, however, means that they are likely to make a better combination with a "people-person," such as an encourager or a mercy giver. The warmth of either of these latter two gifts will balance the giver's detachment. The leader's easiest combination is with the server. Since leaders are endowed with a strong personality, unless they are well developed in their gifting, difficulties may arise with other combinations.

The truth of the matter is that so long as a person with any of the gift packages is walking in the God-kind of love compatibility with others (of any gifting) will not be an insurmountable problem. If someone is abiding in the True Vine, a good relationship with others—even with those who tend to "rub us the wrong way"—is more likely. When people follow the Holy Spirit's lead, He will show them how to maneuver around difficulties and how to work with people and their quirks.

Each gifting has its own particular way of doing things. Take, for example, the case of child rearing. If we are to compare parents who are all Bible-believing Christians, we will discover that teaching-gifted parents will discipline their children in a manner very different from givers, encouragers, prophets, or those with any other gifting. Though all of them may be using the same biblical principles, each gift will apply them differently.

Speaking of children, even "identical" twins will have different spiritual DNA profiles. Do not make the mistake of treating them as if they are the same. It is wiser to use to your understanding of the spiritual DNA of your children to steer them according to the innate needs related to their particular giftings.

And, last but not least, by understanding and appreciating the grace package of your spouse, and treating him or her with love and respect, you will be able to develop a relationship that has the potential to soar. The intimate union God meant for both of you to enjoy can extend far beyond what you may have experienced up to this point in your relationship. That shows just how powerful this understanding of gifting can be when you are operating in wisdom and being led by the Holy Spirit.

Notes

[1] Galatians 5:20.

[2] Strong's Concordance provides the following meanings for the Greek word ek-kheh'-o (G1632), which is translated in Romans 5:5 as "poured": spilled, gushing out, or running greedily out.

[3] Age, sex, upbringing, and cultural differences can be significant factors as well.

[4] Obviously, present-day society's promotion of sexual perversion, falsely claiming it is an issue of "diversity" and "tolerance," is a completely different matter.

[5] Romans 12:3.

Chapter 17

CALLED TO BE YOU!

WHO WILL YOU SERVE?

"Based on the gift they have received, everyone should use it to serve others, as good managers of the varied grace of God." (1 Peter 4:10, HCSB)

You are a reflection of the varied grace of God. Just the intricacy of your one-of-a-kind nature proves it. Most folks will not even stop long enough to consider such things, let alone appreciate the marvel of their making. But you are different.

You must nurture the gifting within. As you purpose to do so, you will come to realize more and more the extent to which you depend on the grace of God. Without the power of His presence in your life, you won't get too far. Developing the potential of your spiritual DNA must be a joint project between you and the Holy Spirit.

God looks on the heart. If you have selfish motives in becoming a "better you" then you will have to improve yourself as a solo effort—you will be on your own. When your motives are in line with God's purposes, however, He will be most willing to help you.

> *Developing the potential of your spiritual DNA must be a joint project between you and the Holy Spirit.*

Two of the greatest hindrances to spiritual growth are an inflated ego and selfishness. Humility, on the other hand, provides a hotbed for cultivating the qualities God desires to bring out in you.

He is the potter, and you are the clay. As you're being conformed to the image that He desires for you, you cannot leap off the wheel and complain to the potter, "I don't agree with this. What are you trying to make of me?" The potter knows best. He has your real interests at heart, for He knows you infinitely better than you know yourself.

Your carnal nature demands that it be served, but you have discovered a higher purpose for your life. The flesh will only put you at odds with God. And when you live according the flesh and its desires, when all is said and done, you will have accomplished very little of the purpose that the Lord had in mind for you from the beginning. Should you decide (and it is always a choice, a choice that only you can make) *not* to heed His voice and pursue the upward calling on your life, at the end of your days He may very well have to include you among those of whom the Apostle Paul wrote *"Their god is their own appetite… and this world is the limit of their horizon."*[1]

Serving God and serving others demonstrates your love for both Him and your fellow man. You have been bought at a high price and you are not your own. He has a claim on you because He redeemed you from the curse.

Your "reasonable service" back to Him is to present yourself as a living sacrifice, making all that you are—spirit, soul, and body—available to your Redeemer-King.[2]

So, whom will you serve—yourself, this world, or your Redeemer-King? Choose rightly—as if all eternity depends on it.

WILL YOU BE REAL?

Because you are now more fully enlightened as to the supernatural nature of your spiritual DNA and the amazing God-given qualities within you, you should also have arrived at a place of greater understanding and deeper appreciation of the *real* you.

The question that applies to some of us is: Why would you want to imitate anyone else? ...personal insecurity? ...a weak self-image? ... lack of confidence?

As you now realize, the Lord thinks highly of you and wants you to be yourself. Growing to be more like Jesus all the time, of course, but still be yourself. In fact, when you grow to be more like Jesus, you will be more "you" as you develop your God-given spiritual DNA.

There is nothing wrong with having good role models. We all need them. But if you are trying to imitate anyone other than Jesus Christ you will eventually find that your efforts end in frustration and disappointment. Becoming a good copy of someone you admire will cause you to be less than what God intends—far short of the original one-of-a-kind that He made you to be.

The better way to prosper spiritually is to look to the One who made you and seek His counsel. When you diligently pursue Him, you will be able to make great strides toward becoming all that you can be.

Becoming firmly rooted in the love of God is the surest solution for overcoming insecurities, poor self-image, and lack of confidence. That happens as you spend time in His presence. What you know to be true from the Scriptures becomes a living reality in your life. You find that His great love overwhelms your doubts and fears. Furthermore, as incredible as it may seem, He really *does* believe in you!

If you haven't been assured of His approval, you may still be seeking approval in the eyes others. If that is your situation, the best you'll be able to do is strive to live up to the reflection of yourself that you see in others' eyes. Even if you were so foolish as to spend precious time looking for that reflection, in the end you would find that it was only

Too many of God's children content themselves with lesser pursuits. They allow the attractions of this world to pull them down from the upward call of Jesus Christ.

a mirage of yourself that you had been chasing all the time.

Reality is based in God. It is, "*… in him we live and move and have our being.*"[3] The project of developing your potential for God's glory is a lifelong pursuit. In time and eternity it is a worthy one that will yield everlasting results.

Too many of God's children content themselves with lesser pursuits. They allow the attractions of this world to pull them down from the upward call of Jesus Christ. When we find ourselves in danger of falling short in this way, we need to remember that the Lord views the work in us as a *great* work.

We need to be as focused as Nehemiah was when his adversaries asked him to meet with them, which would have meant coming down from his God-given assignment of rebuilding the walls of Jerusalem. His response to them was: *"I am engaged in a great work, so I can't come. Why should I stop working to come and meet with you?"*[4] We are surrounded by those who are more than willing to try to lure us to come down to their level of worldly pursuits. It is up to us to take a firm stand and stay focused as Nehemiah did. In our case, God's great project is simply this: working in us and through us so that His purposes are fulfilled.

WILL YOU PRESS ONWARD?

"Not that I have already reached the goal or am already fully mature, but I make every effort to take hold of it because I also have been taken hold of by Christ Jesus." (Philippians 3:12, HCSB)

The Apostle Paul had a wonderfully close relationship with the Lord few others ever have experienced. Because he communed with His Maker in such an intimate way, he was given extraordinary insights. Much of that revelation has come down to us by means of the letters he wrote that eventually became the bulk of the epistles in the New Testament.

And yet, even in the latter days of his ministry, Paul set his sights on becoming more fully mature. He told the Philippians that he was making "every effort" to press on with his goal of becoming "fully mature." What an excellent endeavor!

The Apostle Paul's determination to press onward provides a great example for us all. At whatever stage of spiritual development we are now, there is always room for growth. The enemy of our soul would have us believe otherwise. He wants us to stagnate spiritually and, if it were possible, become retrograde. In fact, backsliding is his specialty!

But every believer has within the ability to become more in God's kingdom. If we have a desire to press on as Paul did—to abide in Jesus Christ and move toward spiritual maturity—we will surely grow in grace.

Believers weren't made to live an ordinary existence. The Lord intends much more for each of His children. He wants us to be extraordinary and to live by His power. Furthermore, He wants us to do exploits.

> *Every believer has the potential to become more in God's kingdom—to abide in Christ and move toward spiritual maturity.*

He has given us *everything* that pertains to life and godliness.[5] He has equipped us in every way. He has given us our spiritual DNA and empowered us to walk in His authority to overcome every obstacle we encounter in life. His grace is sufficient for every situation.

As a believer, you should be at least as dissatisfied with your current level of spiritual maturity as Paul was. God is no respecter of persons— He will do for you as He has done for others. The key is your desire. Are you content to live below your potential? Or do you want to fulfill the destiny that God has planned for you?

WILL YOU DO AS HE SAYS?

The Parable of the Talents clearly demonstrates the Lord's strong desire for us to put to use that which He has given us. We find also that

He is most displeased with those who are supposedly serving Him but take His gifts lightly.

In the parable, the fate of the third servant, the one who buried what the master had given him, is quite revealing. It was bad enough to receive the master's rebuke. But after being called wicked and lazy,[6] that which the master had given him was taken away, and he was to be thrown into outer darkness. The chilling condemnation of the third servant, whom the master viewed as useless,[7] gives us an idea of just how severely the Lord will judge those who fail to put to use that which He has given them. As we can clearly see in this parable, the phrase "use it or lose it" is quite biblical.

If we are half-hearted about the things of God, we are bound for trouble. Those who are lukewarm about the things He cares about meet with His stern disapproval. After all, as His children, our basic motivation in everything we do should be to please Him and bring Him glory. It is for this reason that He chose us and adopted us into His family.

Just to set us straight, Jesus told His disciples in the Upper Room that they did not choose Him but rather it was *He* who chose *them*.[8] What was true for His disciples is just as true for us.

And what is the purpose of Him choosing us? As He told His disciples, it is so that we *"go out and produce fruit and that [our] fruit should remain."* The Lord is not only interested in a relationship; He is also interested in results.

The inherent abilities of our spiritual DNA empowered by God's grace are capable of producing the fruit that He is expecting. They were meant to be put to use for His purposes—to produce fruit for the kingdom. But not just any kind of fruit—fruit that is enduring.

> *The fruit in our lives that the Lord is looking for is produced by the God-kind of love—the sort of love that endures all things and never fails.*

You may be wondering, "What kind of fruit might that be?" It is fruit produced by the God-kind of love—the sort of love that endures all things and never fails. So, whatever is accomplished for His sake out of a motive of the God-kind of love produces the results for which He is looking.

In these Last Days, when so many "followers" of Jesus Christ are content to warm a pew and watch others go about doing the work of the ministry, the question remains: *Will you do as He said? Will you "go" and "produce fruit that will remain?"*

Notes

[1] Philippians 3:19, PNT.

[2] Romans 12:1. Your body is the outward representation of you. All that you are should be presented to Him for service.

[3] Acts 17:28.

[4] Nehemiah 6:3, NLT.

[5] *"For His divine power has given us everything required for life and godliness, through the knowledge of Him who called us by His own glory and goodness."* (2 Peter 1:3, *HCSB*).

[6] See Matthew 25:26.

[7] See Matthew 25:30.

[8] *"You did not choose Me, but I chose you. I appointed you that you should go out and produce fruit and that your fruit should remain, so that whatever you ask the Father in My name, He will give you."* (John 15:16, *HCSB*).

...Learn More About Your Gifting

If you've been blessed to find out more about your spiritual DNA, the book *Called to BE Called to DO*, also by Peter Wollensack, should be of interest. It will provide you with a more in-depth exploration into the gifts that make you who you are!

Here's what a few leaders have said about the book:

Peter Wollensack's easy to read book and the simple to apply Biblical precepts in it will save you much frustration in seeking the means TO DO what we are all "CALLED TO BE." Let me commend Pastor Peter for writing this insightful book, and recommend it to you for reading.

—Rev. Ben Kinchlow, Virginia Beach, Virginia

By discovering your unique spiritual DNA (gifts and callings), and functioning in them, you effectively release Christ Jesus into the world around you and thus fulfill your God given purpose and destiny. Allow this wonderful book to help you accomplish this tremendous feat.

—Dr. Mark Virkler, President, Christian Leadership University, New York

"Called to Be Called to Do" is an absolute must-read for every pastor and minister in the Body of Christ because this teaching is so applicable in the lives of every Christian. The book provides superb insight about the Father's special gifts assigned to all before birth!

—Max O. Flynn, President, Covenant Theological Seminary, Greenville, N.C.

Available at Amazon.com in softcover and Kindle.
Also available in Spanish as *Llamado Para SER Llamado Para HACER*.

Made in the USA
San Bernardino, CA
26 May 2016